Everyday
engagement

katy ridnouer

Everyday engagement

making students and parents
your partners in learning

 | Alexandria, Virginia USA

ASCD®

1703 N. Beauregard St. • Alexandria, VA 22311-1714 USA
Phone: 800-933-2723 or 703-578-9600 • Fax: 703-575-5400
Website: www.ascd.org • E-mail: member@ascd.org
Author guidelines: www.ascd.org/write

Gene R. Carter, *Executive Director;* Judy Zimny, *Chief Program Development Officer,* Nancy Modrak, *Publisher;* Scott Willis, *Director, Book Acquisitions & Development;* Julie Houtz, *Director, Book Editing & Production;* Katie Martin, *Editor;* Greer Wymond, *Senior Graphic Designer;* Mike Kalyan, *Production Manager;* Valerie Sprague, *Desktop Publishing Specialist;* Sarah Plumb, *Production Specialist*

Printed in the United States of America. Cover art © 2011 by ASCD. ASCD publications present a variety of viewpoints. The views expressed or implied in this book should not be interpreted as official positions of the Association.

All web links in this book are correct as of the publication date below but may have become inactive or otherwise modified since that time. If you notice a deactivated or changed link, please e-mail books@ascd.org with the words "Link Update" in the subject line. In your message, please specify the web link, the book title, and the page number on which the link appears.

PAPERBACK ISBN: 978-1-4166-1125-7   ASCD product #109009   n1/11

Also available as an e-book (see Books in Print for the ISBNs).

Quantity discounts for the paperback edition only: 10–49 copies, 10%; 50+ copies, 15%; for 1,000 or more copies, call 800-933-2723, ext. 5634, or 703-575-5634. For desk copies: member@ascd.org.

Library of Congress Cataloging-in-Publication Data
Ridnouer, Katy.
  Everyday engagement : making students and parents your partners in learning / Katy Ridnouer.
    p. cm.
  Includes bibliographical references and index.
  ISBN 978-1-4166-1125-7 (pbk. : alk. paper)   1. Education, Secondary—Parent participation.   2. Community and school.   3. Educational leadership.   I. Title.
  LB1048.5.R535 2011
  371.19'2—dc22

                                                              2010037671

22 21 20 19 18 17 16 15 14 13 12 11   1 2 3 4 5 6 7 8 9 10 11 12

Everyday engagement

Introduction

The Teacher as Everyday Advocate

Wonder, not doubt, is the root of all knowledge.

✳ RABBI ABRAHAM JOSHUA HESCHEL ✳

When I taught my first class of students at Dore Academy in Charlotte, North Carolina, I looked into 15 sets of eyes and thought, "These are my students. I can't wait to see how far I can take them!" Running through my head were all the ways I hoped to connect with them, engage them in meaningful learning activities, and help them develop into thoughtful, capable, educated adults. I wanted to succeed as a teacher so that my students could succeed as learners, and I vowed that together we would take on learning as partners in a great adventure.

The funny thing is, I didn't spare the slightest thought for the people who, next to the students themselves, could have been my closest allies in achieving these objectives: *my students' parents*. Why would I? Nothing in my teacher-certification process had even mentioned parents. I was taught pedagogical strategies, educational philosophy, and lesson planning; I never considered that I could use these same tools to engage parents in their children's academic life. And the truth was, my actual contact with parents was limited. The students attending our K–12 school were dropped off in the morning

1

and picked up in the afternoon, plucked off the steps like ripened tomatoes from a vine. I would call parents occasionally, when there was a problem or a particular success to report, yet I was always uncomfortable during these exchanges. Perhaps it was because the only advice I had received about working with parents came from an administrator colleague, who once whispered to me in the hallway, "Never meet with them alone, Katy. You'll lose your job." This colleague's philosophy when it came to parents? "Give 'em what they want, and you'll get 'em off your back." It was a perspective that cast parents as adversaries instead of partners.

When it came my turn to be "the parent," I was determined *not* to be an adversary at school. I volunteered. I chaperoned. And I realized that parents' roles in school were not limited to victim, complainer, or boss. Parents could make suggestions. We could apply our skills. We could make a difference.

As I worked toward being a partner in my son's academic progress, I began thinking about how each student's academic experience could be enhanced by parent involvement. I also started researching the connections between good teaching practice and the kind of parent involvement that improves student achievement. There was plenty of information available. Since the 1970s, researchers have been documenting the power of home-school connections to enhance student success. School and parent partnerships are associated with higher levels of achievement measured through standardized test scores and with gains in factual, conceptual, critical, and attitudinal aspects of learning (Eccles & Harold, 1993). When parents are involved in their children's education, children may acquire skills and knowledge beyond those they would achieve through school experiences alone (Hoover-Dempsey & Sandler, 1995).

Even as I continued my reading, I delved into some firsthand research by joining the Parent Leadership Network, which meant committing to three weekend training sessions over the course of three months. My fellow trainees and I met with our children's principals and discussed their concerns about parent involvement at the school and particular issues within the school—academic and otherwise. We went on to create project plans that addressed these concerns and made use of both the schools' resources and our personal skill sets.

Guided by the Parent Leadership Network staff, I began to get a clearer sense of the overlap between the elements of successful parent partnership and successful teaching practice. I also realized what parent involvement in schooling could mean for children. Henderson and Berla (1994) tell us that parent partnership benefits students in the following ways:

- A more positive attitude toward school
- Improved academic achievement
- Better behavior in the classroom
- Higher rates of work completion
- Increased participation in classroom activities
- Better attendance

Any educator reading this list is sure to notice that the picture it paints is of a positive, functional, harmonious classroom—the kind of environment we strive to set up for our students and maintain through their collective participation. Once I made that connection, it seemed foolish to continue working alone. Simply put, using engagement practices to partner collaboratively with parents and students alike made much more sense.

Finding a New Solution to a Familiar Challenge

Of course, if facilitating effective parental partnership were simple, all schools would already be doing it. Numerous obstacles stand in the way, from parents' lack of time and know-how, and their perception that schools don't want them around, to teachers' perception that parents don't get involved because they don't care about their own children's academic success. According to the 2006 MetLife Survey of the American Teacher, new teachers consider engaging and working with parents their greatest challenge, more so than classroom management, organizing a new classroom, or obtaining supplies. In fact, parent involvement in learning is the area they feel the *least* prepared to respond to during their first year of teaching. Not surprisingly, fewer than half of the new teachers surveyed were satisfied with their relationship with parents.

It is time for a change. It is time to look at parent partnership in a different way, using the lens of engagement. Encouraging parent partnership doesn't mean tallying the number of hours parents are in the school building each week or teaching parents how to teach reading. What it means is cultivating a welcoming atmosphere for parents, just as we create a welcoming atmosphere for our students. It means giving parents comfortable and significant ways to participate in the schooling process in the same way we aim to give our students meaningful and appropriate work to help them master academic goals and other classroom challenges.

Meaningful Engagement

One of the most valuable lessons I've learned as a teacher is that all students need to feel seen and known. Before they will fully engage their minds in the classroom, they need to believe that their teacher has an understanding of who they are. Involving parents in and out of the classroom provides a way for teachers to complete the full picture of who students are by capturing the personal details that can fall through the sieve of students' school records, anecdotes from previous teachers, and the face students present in the classroom.

For me, the real breakthrough came when I realized that parents, too, need to be seen and known. The same five elements that are essential to engaging students in the educational process are critical to engaging their parents:

1. *Laying the groundwork for engagement:* Recognizing that each student and each parent is a unique individual and finding a way for every person to contribute to a positive learning environment.

2. *Communicate invitations:* Maintaining a welcoming attitude and inviting both student and parent participation in the learning community.

3. *Cultivating interpersonal responses:* Considering what students and parents are willing and able to give of themselves and providing appropriate support and encouragement.

4. *Dealing effectively with engagement challenges:* Anticipating and handling setbacks and complications related to connecting with both students and parents.

5. *Extending the learning community:* Tapping outside resources.

Being the Difference, Being the Advocate

The approach I outline in this book reflects my own experience as a teacher and a parent, as well as the experiences of my students, children, friends, and colleagues. As noted, my writing has been further informed by the insights of the Parent Leadership Network and by research on parent and student involvement. What I advocate here is in many ways an extension of my first book, *Managing Your Classroom with Heart* (Ridnouer, 2006), which explored how a compassionate teacher can bring out the best in students. Teachers who focus this same compassion on parents will be able to initiate productive and rewarding conversations about forming home-school connections that support student learning.

An advocate is a person who supports or promotes the interests of another, and that is what a teacher is doing when he or she works to engage students and their parents as partners in a positive, learning-focused classroom community. An advocate is also one who promotes a cause, and I believe every teacher must be an advocate for student and parent engagement in learning, and for learning in general. They must promote it actively; they must embed these efforts into their classroom practice on an everyday basis. Some students and parents will be prone to engagement—easy to reach, easy to know, and eager to be involved in the classroom—due to the very nature of who they are. Other students and parents are the exact opposite. I believe it is up to the teacher to cast a net wide enough to pull in students and parents—those who are naturally inclined toward engagement and those who reject the traditional methods of engagement.

Each of this book's five parts focuses on one of the key elements of meaningful engagement, identifying and answering specific questions you may have, and offering strategies for tackling the associated challenges. Taken together, these elements provide a stable groundwork for a collaborative partnership among schools, students, and parents—a partnership that, once established, becomes as much of a part of the classroom environment as curricula, pencils, and paper. And from that point, the question for students and parents is not *if* they will be engaged in classroom learning, but *how* they will choose to engage, *how far* that engagement will take them, and *what else* is possible.

Every teacher has the power to be a tremendously positive force in the lives of their students. The fact that you are reading this book suggests you share this belief, and I hope that the questions asked and strategies explored in the pages ahead will be helpful in your work. Let's get started.

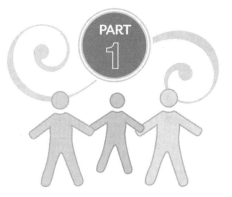

The Groundwork for Engagement

A sense of humor, personal quirks, and passions are unique traits that can be found in both students and their parents. Effective teachers notice which activities make their students' eyes light up and which challenges cause their foreheads to wrinkle with confusion. Parents can give us the same clues, helping us to deduce what generates excitement and what generates excuses about their becoming engaged in their children's academic world.

Once teachers see students and parents as people—and thereby come to know them—they can set appropriate expectations and provide effective support for school involvement.

Seeing the Person Before You

Wouldn't it be great if all students entered the classroom eager to complete every assignment and ready to excel at every challenge? Actually, I don't think that it would be. For me, the best part of teaching is seeing students grasp a new concept or push themselves beyond what they thought were their boundaries.

Every teacher has the opportunity to be that person in the lives of their students—the person who instills in them the desire to know more and do more, who encourages them to take a risky but rewarding path, and who helps them persevere instead of allowing them to quit when they face challenges and become frustrated or overwhelmed. But when it comes to being advocates for our students—doing our best to help them connect with material and excel academically, socially, and personally—teachers often overlook or underutilize key partners: the students' parents. Forging a partner-ship with both students and their parents is not always easy, but it is essential to education. Taking the time to see each child and each parent before you as individuals will give you insight into how best to include them in the learning process.

This partnership with parents can provide the motivational sup-port that will encourage *parent involvement* to evolve into the more symbiotic relationship of *parent engagement*. Larry Ferlazzo (2009) differentiates between the two terms this way:

> When schools *involve* parents they are leading with their insti-tutional self-interest and desires—school staff are leading with their *mouths*. When schools *engage* parents they are leading with the parents' self-interests (their wants and dreams) in an effort to develop a genuine partnership. In this instance, school staff are leading with their *ears*. (para. 3)

Research confirms that when parents and teachers work together, students benefit (Redding, Langdon, Meyer, & Sheley, 2004). My aim is to clarify the "how" of engaging both students and parents in the pursuit of learning and achievement. Creating and sustain-ing opportunities for effective involvement depends on you, the teacher, understanding and overcoming the academic, social, and emotional barriers to student and parent engagement so that you can build the kind of positive, collaborative relationships that will help your students meet curricular goals.

In this chapter, we will look at some strategies you can use to help you see your students and their parents as the people they are. Here are the key questions we'll consider:

1. What does "engagement" really mean, and what are some first steps for engaging students and parents?

2. What does it mean to "understand" your students and their parents?

3. How will understanding your students and their parents help you engage them?

The Real Meaning of "Engagement" and Some First Steps

Engagement happens when students are involved in activities that spark a desire in them. Finding out what these activities are requires some research, observation, and interaction on your part to ensure that students not only learn what they are required to learn, but that they personalize what they learn and can build on it in the future.

The process of engaging parents in activities in and out of school is similar to that of engaging students. You just have to tweak the materials and the information to serve parent interests and parent needs. In this way you will pique parents' desire to see how deep an impact they can have on their children's achievement.

Student Engagement as the Nexus of Understanding and Instructional Intent

Every teacher strives to achieve the goal of student engagement—which I see as the moment when students' understanding meets the lesson plan and shakes hands... when distractions and outside concerns recede and students are focused on their learning.

Of course, classroom management practices and carefully crafted assignments are necessary components of student engagement, but it's also important that students understand that being successful in your classroom means they need to work to bridge the gap between their knowledge base and the day's lesson. You, as their education guide, should not only expect student engagement but also welcome it and usher it in every day. Now, some strategies.

▶ Try to figure out what your students are (really) thinking

The combination of your understanding of the subject matter and your knowledge of what helps and hinders your students' learning process, called pedagogical content knowledge (Cochran, 1997), is the key to effective instruction. Maintaining an awareness of the emotional messages students send themselves as they move through the learning process provides you with key information on how to best reach them and teach them.

As much as we like to tell ourselves that our students are hanging on our every word, we know that everything we say plays in counterpoint to the commentary running through their heads: *"OK, I think Ms. Davis is saying that what she's doing is another way to balance an equation." "What? Huh? I have no idea what Mrs. Reyes is talking about." "Here we go again. I guess I really am stupid. Why even bother listening anymore?"* This internal talk is a kind of virtual steering wheel, but it's important to remember that it can point students toward success just as easily as it can point them toward failure.

The research of Bernard Weiner (1994) offers insight into these internal student messages. He found that the reasons students give for their academic failure and success actually predict the feelings they hold toward their academic abilities and determine how they will approach future academic tasks. When Weiner asked failing students to explain why they were failing, they typically attributed it to one of four reasons:

- They weren't smart or capable enough.
- They knew how difficult a task was and failed to do the work necessary to complete it.
- They thought the work was just too hard.
- They blamed external factors beyond their control, such as luck or home circumstances.

When Weiner asked successful students about the reasons for their success, they responded with these reasons:

- They were born smart.
- They tried hard.
- The task was easy.
- They were lucky or the teacher liked them.

Note that out of these four reasons for success, there is only one that students can control—trying hard. Happily, there is much a teacher can do to influence the effectiveness of this reason for success. Talk to your students about the value of hard work. Devote class time to discussing Weiner's research to help students build a frame of reference for the difficulties they should expect to face when they study. They might be like many students, erroneously believing that "smart people" or "good students" don't have to struggle; therefore, if they find themselves struggling with a task, they must not be "smart enough." The better they understand that struggle is a reality for most learners, the more willing they will be to accept it as part of the learning process.

I can suggest some responses to Weiner's four excuses for failure.

▶ Respond to "I'm just not smart enough" by changing students' perspective

Failing students who receive an *F* on a test and say, "I'm just not smart enough" are trying to convince themselves that they are incapable of completing the task. Meanwhile, the message they are really sending is, "I've learned so many other things more quickly, and I don't understand why I should be having such much trouble with this."

Students need to know that their self-definition of what they can or cannot do isn't fixed; they can change it. All of us have innate skills and strengths we can tap to bridge the difference between what we can achieve or understand easily and what's expected of us. Look for opportunities to illustrate how this works by giving students who struggle in one area a chance to use their strengths in another. For example, a class chatterbox could lead the part of a math review that he or she is particularly good at, or a quiet student could work one-on-one with a compassionate classmate to shore up the breach in his or her understanding of the material.

When you talk to your students during lunch and between classes, discuss sports, politics, and school events. This gives them opportunities to develop their voice in subjects they are comfortable discussing. It also lets you model how a person goes about expanding knowledge. During these discussions, when you have questions about a topic, ask them! Between conversations, seek out information and share what you have learned during the next conversation. Stress the satisfaction that comes from success achieved through hard work.

▶ Respond to "It was just too much" by teaching the power of perseverance

When students are aware of the steps they need to take to complete a task but choose not to take those steps, they are choosing failure over hard work. When you pass back a failed test, you might hear them say, "I would've had to review the entire textbook to pass that final!" These students need to learn the value of perseverance. Find a day when you have 10 or 15 minutes to lead a discussion about the definition of perseverance and the value of it. Make it clear that perseverance means working until a task is complete instead of attempting something and quitting when it gets difficult. Ask for student input and create a list of steps that need to be taken to complete a task they are familiar with, such as getting ready for school in the morning, learning how to ride a bike, or tying their shoes. Then discuss whether or not the effort of completing all of the steps was worth the end result.

▶ Respond to "It was too hard" by zeroing in on the stumbling block

Students who rely on this excuse typically say things like, "I have never understood math, and I never will!" These words are just shadows of what students really mean. The truth is that they haven't found a way to connect with the material and are afraid that if they have to struggle, they just might not be all that bright. Help them recognize struggle as a sign that they need to try learning this material in a different way. If students squirm during a lecture, maybe they are visual learners who need to see the information to digest it. Suggest that they take notes, draw time lines, or design symbols for the new information you are relaying to them. Putting the responsibility on the students sends the message that they are capable of managing their own academic success.

▶ Respond to "It's not *my* fault!" with compassion

The last excuse, in which outside factors control the student's success, can be heard in statements such as, "The teacher likes all the blonde-haired girls and gives them easier work." There is usually something else going on when students make these kinds of statements. They want to act like their struggles aren't a big deal, but failure is a big deal whether on a quiz, a test, or even a homework grade. By responding compassionately to student failure, you will help students build a bridge and get over their struggle.

The inner workings of students' personal lives sometimes cloud their judgment. It is the teacher's job to see the difficulty without judging the cloud. One of my students, Michael, announced in class one day that the reason he wasn't doing his work was because he was a poor kid from the country whom nobody expected to finish school anyway. He sounded to me like a kid on the verge of dropping out. That night, I called Michael at home to talk to him about my concern about the statements he had made in class. He was initially very quiet, and then he admitted that he had started using drugs again and was really confused about the direction his life was taking. He went on to say that so many people were telling him what to do that he was stuck.

I let him talk and then told him that I wasn't going to be one of those people who told him what to do. Instead, I told him the facts. He could still pass my class, and I was willing to work with him if he ran into difficulty. I said that I hoped I would see him tomorrow and reminded him of the supplies he needed in class. He thanked me, and I hung up the phone not really knowing if I would ever see him again.

The next day, there Michael was, sitting in his usual seat left of center, smiling. I smiled back. He worked hard to complete everything he had missed, and he ended up passing with a *C*. At the end of the semester, Michael gave me this letter:

Dear Ms. Ridnouer,

Thank you for reaching out to me personally and telling me to not give up. I will remember you always as a wonderful teacher and also a person. I want to let you know that I will keep my head up and try to make you proud about our achievements.

Thank you,

Michael R.

Michael had already made me proud. He had swallowed his own pride, dug in, and did the hard work of figuring how to finish what he had started.

At some point in their academic career, all students need help finishing what they've started. You can provide the link that will help them connect effectively to each of their fields of knowledge.

Parent Engagement as a Wide-Ranging Menu

A mom leading kindergarteners from the bus lot to their classroom. A dad talking to students about his job on Career Day. A grandmother leading a poetry reading session. A mom researching the per-student cost of an 8th grade field trip to the state capitol building. All of these are examples of parent engagement. None is "better" than any other. Each is a simply a different way of being engaged and reflects the parent's comfort level, personal circumstances, and interests.

Joyce Epstein (2001) has identified a framework covering six types of parent involvement: *parenting, communicating, volunteering, learning at home, decision making,* and *collaborating with community.*

(See Figure 1.1 for a letter to parents that elaborates on how they can contribute within the context of these categories.) Finding out what parents believe "parent involvement" to mean and where they would feel comfortable contributing their service will help you create appropriate invitations for parents. The letter in Figure 1.1 could serve as a schoolwide communication or, with some modification, could be used by individual teachers.

Engaging parents in their child's education—whether in or out of the classroom—helps students receive the message that school is important and that everybody plays a role in teaching students. When parents are engaged, they begin to trust that the teacher cares about them and their child. This trust builds parents' confidence in the teacher's ability to meet the individual needs of students. It also breeds a willingness to become involved at a higher level, because parents trust the teacher will offer them volunteer opportunities that fit their own skill set.

What It Means to "Understand" Your Students and Their Parents

Effective teachers strive to understand families and provide invitations tailored to the families' strengths and weaknesses. Both efforts involve doing a little research. Find out the demographics of your student population, including their parents' economic levels, race, marital status, and religion. Learn about their everyday habits and interests, as well as the challenges they face. This understanding will help determine the type of engagement you can successfully cultivate. For example, be mindful of the family's expectations of how children should interact with adults and how involved they believe families should be with their children's education. You might have some parents who don't believe they have a place in the school environment and other parents who need to be shown how to moderate their involvement. The better you understand your families, the better you will be able to guide them.

Figure 1.1

Sample Parent Handout: Involvement Information Sheet

Parent Involvement: What It Means in Our School

1. *Parenting.* The most fundamental way you can be involved in your child's education is to support and promote your child as a student. Workshops and presentations on parenting topics will be available throughout the year.

2. *Communicating.* We pledge to provide you with meaningful information about your child's progress and about events going on in school, such as testing programs, field trips, after-school activities, and opportunities for extra help and enrichment. In turn, we seek information from you about your child's strengths, talents, and needs. We ask that you keep your child's teacher informed of absences, medication issues, and family changes. If you are not getting the information you need from school, or if you have information to share that will improve our ability to teach your child, please contact your child's teacher.

3. *Volunteering.* We need your help to provide a safe, nurturing learning environment inside and outside the classroom. Please consider your areas of interest and choose a volunteer opportunity from the list that concludes this form.

4. *Learning at home.* Your child will see himself or herself as a student if you consistently make homework a high priority. Providing encouragement and a well-lit homework spot is all the assistance your child should need.

5. *Decision making.* We need your input in school decisions, ranging from managing behavior on the school bus to implementing a plan for remediating poorly performing students. Consider joining the PTA and our school's leadership team.

6. *Collaborating with community.* Help us create a bridge from the community to our school by sharing contacts who might be able to contribute services, volunteers, supplies, or a monetary donation.

Please let us know how you would like to be involved.

Parenting
____ Participate in a parenting workshop.
     Area of interest: _____
____ Attend a parenting seminar.
     Area of interest: _____
____ Organize materials in parent center.

Communicating
_____ Offer translation services. Language(s): _____
_____ Assist with school newsletter.
_____ Photograph school activities.
_____ Call parents about attendance or an upcoming event.
_____ Distribute school and curricular information.
_____ Prepare bulletin boards.

Volunteering
_____ Tutor a student.
_____ Be a lunch buddy.
_____ Work with small groups.
_____ Do clerical work in the classroom.
_____ Chaperone field trips.
_____ Help with special events.
_____ Be a guest speaker.
_____ Greet visitors at the school.
_____ Shelve books in the media center.

Learning at home
_____ Create student packets at home.
_____ Cut out and collate activity sheets.
_____ Participate with your child in interactive homework assignments.
_____ Manage phone/e-mail/texting tree in an emergency.
_____ Support your child's daily study habits.

Decision making
_____ Participate on a leadership team, parent organization, or committee.
       Area of interest: _____
_____ Become a community representative.
_____ Collect and distribute information about school board meetings and
       decisions.

Collaborating with community
_____ Recruit community members for volunteer opportunities.
_____ Solicit community funding.
_____ Collect and distribute information about community programs.
_____ Collect and distribute information about services that could serve school
       community.
_____ Make school aware of community service projects available to students.
_____ Network with alumni to support school activities.

Many students and parents will be agreeable to your invitations and happily tuck into assignments. Others will refuse. It would be easy to get mad at the refusers and think negatively about them. Instead, stick to the plan of being an advocate for students and parents. Respond with compassion to those students and parents who reject your invitations, reminding yourself that there are often reasons for such refusals. To find those reasons, you need to seek understanding.

Understanding Your Students

Whether this is your first year of teaching or your fourteenth, you are most likely in this field because you care about your students. This caring is buttressed by a faith in your students—a belief based on a feeling, a hope that your understanding of your students will help them become their best selves.

▶ Look at student behavior as expression of basic needs

William Glasser's (1998) Choice Theory proposes that students have basic needs to be fulfilled in the classroom, including survival, love and belonging, power, freedom, and fun. Students who are making poor academic and behavioral choices are attempting to fulfill one of these basic needs. Reframing my students' problems this way helps me to respond compassionately to my students, as it takes the blame and the shame away from the flunking or misbehaving student. Once I work out which of the basic needs the student is trying to fulfill, I can cultivate a response that will meet the student's needs in an alternative, positive way.

Here are a few examples of student behavior, the corresponding basic need being expressed, and some suggestions for how to positively respond.

Behavior: defiance; basic need: survival

Defiant behavior is maddening; because of this, it is tempting to get angry when a student disrupts class or intentionally breaks class rules. The behavior is the student's response to what he or she sees as a confining situation. Likening the student to a caged animal might help you feel some compassion, and your anger will dissipate.

Find a time when the two of you can talk one on one. Ask questions such as "What's bothering you?" and "How can I help?" Ask for input on an effective way for you to respond to his or her defiance and come up with a response that makes you both happy. Eventually, the student will see that while your expectations are high, you will help them meet or surpass those goals.

Behavior: making excuses; basic need: love and belonging

Students make excuses as a means of getting attention from you. The excitement these students get from the teacher being disappointed in them for "accidentally" pushing a classmate or having to go to their locker or call a parent for "forgotten" work is well worth the negative consequences of making a poor choice. Ask yourself: Is there a learning difficulty the student is trying to hide? Is the student lonely and in need of more attention? Is he or she a gifted student who finds the work to be a waste of time?

Listen for clues and respond to excuses with quick, pat responses. For example, when a student says, "I forgot my homework" or "My book is in my locker," respond with "Bring it in tomorrow" or "Borrow my book." The student's response will give you clues as to what he or she needs. If the student says, "Let me run to the office to call my mom," you know that he or she needs attention. "May I run to my locker?" tells you that the student wants to avoid the lesson because it is either too hard or too easy. In either case, respond with "No," and then plan a time when you can confer with the student, and perhaps the parents, too, to respond to the larger issue. A student who needs more attention can be assigned as a buddy to someone else in the class, be given a class job, or be given extra-credit assignments. A student whose academic needs aren't being met needs to be referred to the school counselor for diagnosis.

Behavior: silliness; basic need: power

The student who reads a story aloud in an I-just-sucked-helium voice or cracks jokes in the middle of the lesson might as well wear a t-shirt that says, "I'm the REAL teacher." He or she wants you and the class to know that the student is in charge. If you respond by yelling or isolating the student, you are bolstering that idea.

Surprise the disruptive student and the rest of the class by making disruption part of the class lesson. Talk about disruptions as they relate to the subject matter. In science class, for example, you might discuss how unnatural interruptions affect cell reproduction; in social studies, how unwelcome arrivals affect societies; in math, how adding an extra number changes an equation; and in English, how a silly character influences a story.

One student of mine, Craig, was ingenious at cracking a joke just when I reaching the main point of a lesson. When I was teaching *Romeo and Juliet* and asked, "Now why would Romeo 'cross the road,' as it were, and fall in love with Juliet?" it was Craig who quipped, "To get to the other side."

Good one, I thought, and then I asked Craig, "Who was on the other side?"

He surprised everyone by answering, "The Capulets. And anyway, Romeo loved her, man. He didn't care what family she was in."

He was right, of course, and we were back on track with the lesson. In addition, Craig had shown me that love was something that was important to him. I tucked this essential information into the back of my mind and waited for a chance to use it to engage him further in class.

I didn't have to wait long. The next day, I met him in the hallway before class and asked him, "Who are you most like? Your mom or your dad?"

"Why?"

"I'm just curious who you take after."

"My dad, I guess. He's the smooth one."

"Oh yeah?"

"Yeah. He's always dressed to the nines."

I appraised Craig's own ensemble (Tommy Hilfiger shirt and jeans and bright white sneakers) and said, "So are you. You always look put together."

"Thanks, Ms. Ridnouer."

Discussing Craig's beloved father and underscoring their similarities was a way to help him see that he was already directing his power; he didn't need to steal it in my classroom.

Behavior: teasing; basic need: fun

Students who point out another student's buzz cut or that the new kid is overweight are looking to fill a need for fun. When students first begin teasing, they make these comments to entertain themselves and others. They think what they are saying is quite witty, and they are proud of themselves. Why shouldn't they be? They believe that they have the chutzpah to say what everyone else just wishes they had the nerve to say. It's only in hindsight or in a discussion with a teacher or a parent that students will understand that their words hurt the feelings of the person they were teasing, and they'll often try to laugh it off with "I'm only telling the truth!" and "Oh, that kid has no sense of humor."

Discuss how healthy humor involves jokes that both teller and listener can enjoy without getting their feelings hurt. Lend these students a joke book and assign them the task of telling you five favorite jokes by the end of the week. Meet again after you have had a chance to analyze the type of joke that they like. Find the higher-level attribute that the jokes embody. Does a student like the how-animals-are-like-people jokes? Does another like the ones that rely on wordplay? Does another appreciate irony? When you meet again, tell a teasing student that you are concerned with how such jokes affect classroom relationships and that you are afraid the student will lose friends because of the jokes. Point out the type of joke that the student found funny in the joke book and encourage him or her to memorize a few of those types of jokes to have at the ready when the time is appropriate for joke telling.

The behavior will not come to a full stop immediately, so ask students how they would like you to respond when the habit of teasing starts up again. Raise your eyebrows? Wink? Clear your throat? Start walking toward the student? Tell the student to stop? Tap his or her shoulder? Ask how his or her dad is doing? Personalizing the signal with the student's input will help bring positive change to his or her behavior.

Behavior: hyperactivity; basic need: freedom

Oftentimes, hyperactive students annoy themselves with their behavior as much as they annoy their classmates, but they don't know how to stop the touching, tapping, and squirming. The behavior that started as a way to free themselves of the shackles of school has become a habit that has gotten out of hand. Now they need help reining in the behavior. Try to develop a system that suits both the student and yourself.

For my student Ronnie, drumming on his desk was his response to what he considered a boring lesson. Having also noticed that he frequently patted people on the back and gesticulated a lot when he spoke, I figured a kinesthetic response would be an effective one for Ronnie. I walk around a lot when I am teaching, so it's not unusual for me to be in the back of the class as much as I am in the front. When Ronnie began his drumming, I would maintain my course around the classroom and place my hands on his as I passed his desk. This quick, silent response was all the reminder he needed. His drumming never stopped 100 percent, but I was aiming for improvement, not perfection, and a considerable decrease was a victory for me and a big relief to the students sitting near Ronnie.

Other responses for hyperactive students include determining a signal that only you and the student are aware of. Holding your hand up in the "stop" position or winking can work, as can taping a stop sign on the student's desk and pointing to it. Look for a way that will help students see that they don't need freedom from the physical confines of the classroom, they need freedom from boredom. Only they can control that.

Understanding Your Students' Parents

Parents who choose to not become engaged in their child's school community make that choice for a variety of reasons. Before you make your plans for reaching out to parents, consider the reasons they might stay away.

As far as parent's physical absence from the school building, that's often a simple matter of a child growing up. At the elementary level, students are usually thrilled to see their parents at school events. Once students reach middle and high school, however, the prospect of seeing their parents at school can be mortifying, and they may even ask their moms and dads not to embarrass them with their presence. Given that the parents are dealing with a new environment, working with new teachers, and discovering the complexities of having an adolescent at home, the natural reaction of many parents is to simply back off and leave schooling to the school.

Consider also that parents refrain from taking part in school-related activities because they don't have access to transportation or to child care for younger children, don't have flexible workplaces, or don't have the funds to cover field trip fees for both their child and themselves. A single parent who is working two jobs to support her family simply may not have any free time to offer but might welcome suggestions from you on how she could still stay engaged in her child's school life.

Another significant step in understanding your students' parents is recognizing their valuable attributes and how they contribute to the growth of their child. Epstein and Dauber (1991) found that teachers who view parents as a child's "first teacher" are more likely to invite them to become active participants in their children's education.

▶ Provide opportunities for parents to give you background information

Give parents the "In one million words or less..." homework assignment: "In one million words or less, tell me what I need to know about your child and your family. Include your dreams, fears, hopes, and doubts." Parents could provide information that would take you weeks to deduce on your own: one child might need to use his muscles by walking around while learning math concepts; another might need some extra patience because she is struggling emotionally after the death of her grandmother. This information will help you gauge a student's academic progress and give parents the opportunity to share their hopes and dreams for their child. Provide a section for the parent to write their contact details so that you can send a follow-up thank-you and keep the contact information on hand for future reference. This assignment can give you an idea of the value that each family places on education and insight into how to approach them if a concern arises.

Just as every student responds with varying levels of enthusiasm and depth, parents will respond in various ways to this assignment. Assign it anyway and accept the information as pieces of a treasure map leading to academic achievement. Some parents might find the assignment intrusive; other parents might not respond at all. Follow up with these parents via another means of communication. No matter what they think of the assignment before you call or e-mail, they will think more highly of you as their child's teacher once they see you make the extra effort to get in touch with them.

This kind of assignment also serves as evidence for both students and their parents that you, as their teacher, care about them and want to know them. Most parents love to talk about their children and will warm up to anyone who asks about them. Teachers can build on this warm feeling by offering subsequent parent involvement opportunities that appeal to their interests and qualifications.

How an Understanding of Students and Parents Will Help You Engage Them

After collecting and digesting the information about your students and their parents, you might wonder how to use it to teach more effectively and gain parental support. First of all, don't expect that you will be able to connect the dots of each student's life experience to your lesson plan and every parent's concern to your parent engagement plan. Instead, look for patterns in both your students and their parents. Elementary teachers can focus on general interests that most of the students display—maybe a love of soccer or Yu-Gi-Oh, or an interest in learning to type—and use these topics in grammar worksheets, math problems, and essay requirements. Middle and high school teachers can focus on the elements of their subject area that their students struggle with and pair them with student interests. Giving students options in how to respond to assignments will show your willingness to consider their preferences in schoolwork, and schoolwork that appeals to students will increase their engagement.

Understanding Students to Increase Your Motivational Power

Successful students often devise a plan of action for themselves when they are completing homework or preparing for a test. They know how to digest new information and articulate it in their own way. Less successful students might complete their homework and read over review questions, but they don't have a plan to make the information their own. Consequently, they don't learn much. The more you know and understand about them, the more effective you can be in helping them draw connections between who they are and what the curriculum may have to offer them. It's a matter of opening their eyes and giving them the tools they need to think about how they approach learning and how they might regulate their in-class responses.

▶ Teach metacognition

Metacognition is thinking about thinking. Using metacognitive tools can benefit both student engagement and student performance. Begin a discussion on metacognition by asking students to write their answers to the following questions:

- How do you learn best?
- What gets in the way of your learning?
- What kind of information do you absorb easily?
- What kind of information is difficult to understand?

I teach my students to engage their metacognitive skills by continuously asking them to analyze what they already know, their plan for completing this task, and their work when they are done. For example, when we prepare for a test, I discuss what will be on the test and suggest a few ways they could review. When I hand out graded tests, I lead a group discussion about the test's content. We discuss question such as "What was my main focus on this test?" or "Why do you suppose that I focused on that topic?" or "How would you prepare for this test differently?" Pushing students to think about the "how" of their schoolwork makes their efforts more intentional. Instead of settling on an excuse of "I'm just dumb" when they receive a bad grade, they can decide to participate more in class, become mindful of the best environment to study in, and create strategies for problem solving that reflect their learning style.

▶ Teach self-regulating skills

Everybody feels like skipping when the sun is shining, but most of us don't skip when we're in school because we know that isn't the right place for such physical exuberance. We all want to blurt out answers and go to the bathroom right when we need to, but we don't because we've learned self-regulating behaviors.

Students who learn how to regulate their behavior are able to analyze how they learn and improve the learning process with each study session. Lead discussions or create journal assignments about behaviors that might get in the way of students' learning, such as talking during class, daydreaming, or tapping their feet. A study conducted by Lane, Pierson, and Givner (2003) found that elementary, middle, and high school teachers rated self-control and cooperation skills as essential to success. They concluded, "These are skills that can, and should, be taught explicitly upon initial school entry" (p. 427). Define cooperation for your classroom so that your students know what kind of behavior you expect. Let them know how to be physically and mentally present. Should they sit in a certain way? Respond to lessons in a certain way? Take notes? Ask questions? When are they allowed to talk? Go to the bathroom? Ask about homework? The clearer you are with these rules, the better they will be able to follow them.

▶ Be mindful of your classroom responses

Children as young as 5 years old are capable of deducing a teacher's opinion of their ability based on the teacher's emotional reaction to a student's performance (Weiner, Graham, Stern & Lawson, 1982). If a student answers a question incorrectly and the teacher becomes angry, children deduce that the teacher is angry because the student did not study enough. If the teacher responds with sympathy when the student answers incorrectly, children deduce that the teacher must believe that the student doesn't have the ability to understand the material. In other words, if you get angry, the child believes you are angry because the child could have controlled the outcome and chose not to. Conversely, students believe that if you feel sorry for them, then they should feel sorry for themselves, too, because they must not be that bright.

Effective educators remember that they're "on stage" and use a wide array of responses to their students. Responding with the intensity of anger but the compassion of pity is a pitch that students respond well to. You do this when you identify a positive aspect of a student's work when he or she is struggling. However, what you point out to the student as a sign of growth has to in fact show growth in understanding. Students know that comments on neatness do not reflect on an increase in their knowledge of fractions. Look for areas of growth. Point out that a student only missed three problems instead of seven, showing that the students' studying efforts are paying off. In a multistep problem, highlight the fact that the student completed three out of four steps correctly. These responses offer the benefit of high expectations without the negative emotions that arise when teachers respond with anger or pity.

▶ Plant the seeds of motivation

People with a common goal have a straight line to walk to success. Create a class goal with your students and reinforce the goal with a few of these ideas:

• Create a class motto by presenting a list of action verbs that groups of students can use to create a motivational class statement. Have the students vote on the motto, and then post it around the room.

• Collect quotes that exemplify the qualities that you are looking for and post them around the room in a font that students can read from their desks.

• Hang up posters that visually inspire students through interesting photography and messages.

• Assure your students that in order for them to learn, they must be uncertain. They have to be willing to leap into that uncomfortable zone of confusion in order for learning to take place. Let them know that it is OK to feel unsettled by new ideas or to be unsure about how a lesson meshes with previous lessons. Encourage them to recognize this unsettled feeling as a gift, a sign that they are learning something new.

• If you teach younger students, post pictures of faces that exhibit different emotions around the room, and refer to these posters when interacting with your students. Motivating emotions could be put on one side of the room and dispiriting emotions on the other to help students visualize crossing from one emotional side to the other. Alternately, you could pair differing types of emotions to help students see how the negative can lead to the positive. For example, you could pair frustration and inspiration, boredom and excitement, embarrassment and pride, and sadness and exhilaration.

Understanding Parents to Guide Your Outreach

Teachers have a distinct advantage over parents in understanding the social and academic parameters appropriate for a particular age group. The sheer number of students they have the opportunity to work with each year gives them an understanding of what is normal and what is worrisome. Once you understand what behaviors or study skills your students' parents are concerned about, you can communicate how to address their concerns at home and at school.

▶ Share your age-group expertise

While you should always address specific concerns that parents share with you, you can ameliorate these concerns by providing general information to parents about behaviors and responsibilities that are developmentally appropriate for the age group that you teach. Sharing this will help parents understand the specific challenges their child faces and what allowances they should make based on their child's age and development.

▶ Offer a variety of tools for various types of involvement

Parents might believe that because they've never been involved in their child's school, or haven't been involved since elementary school, that it is too late to make contact. You can change that belief. In fact, you have a responsibility to develop ways for parents to get involved that support curricular, family, and student needs. You have the resources and the knowledge to provide parents with tools to support their children effectively.

Create a regular place for parents to look for suggestions on how to support their children. This could be a class website, weekly e-mails, or a class newsletter. Suggestions might include the following:

• "Maintain family time for regular discussion of school-related triumphs and challenges."

• "Enforce consistent rules to create safe mental and physical boundaries for your child."

• "Show that education is important by holding high expectations and setting aside study time each night."

You can also take personal action to improve the lives of your students' families. These might include the following:

• Establishing a classroom library for parents with materials on child development, at-home learning activities, and discipline strategies.

• Visiting the homes of the most reluctant parents to provide personal contact, share information, and discuss any questions and concerns they might have.

• Designing workshops for parents based on their concerns.

• Developing tip sheets on how parents can help their child succeed in school.

The payoff is worthwhile. Patrikakou (2004) reports that when parents expressed the belief that their child would go far in school, the children performed accordingly. Students had a clearer perception of parent expectations, spent more time on homework, and achieved more academically. And the effects go beyond academics: Simon (2001) found that students were more likely to report being better behaved and coming to class prepared when they reported talking with their parents about school and college planning. When parents mirror the school's message about behavior, class preparedness, and planning for the future, they motivate students to make positive decisions both in and out of school.

Sow Now, Reap the Rewards Later

Planting seeds of change will help students nurture themselves as learners and make their education an individual process that will become knowledge that they can own forever. Ralph Waldo Emerson stated in *Self-Reliance*, "In every work of genius we recognize our own rejected thoughts: they come back to us with a certain alienated majesty." This is very similar to Kahlil Gibran's message: "No man can reveal to you aught but that which already lies half asleep in the dawning of your knowledge." That's why ideas seem to click in our brains when they make sense—it's the effect of two ideas embracing each other. If students cannot connect with an idea, they are just memorizing, not learning. Take the time to figure out what your students know best and how you can connect this knowledge with the current curricula.

As you encourage students to figure out their learning process and use that knowledge to "hook into" their education, advocate for parents to embark on the engagement process as well by becoming active members in their child's academic life. Empowering parents respects their role in their child's life and lays the groundwork for future engagement.

Invitations

Students and parents are very attuned to the way you present yourself in person, in speech, and in writing. They can decide in the blink of an eye what your words and actions "mean," and they will respond accordingly.

Effective teachers understand that students and parents bring their own points of view to every interaction, whether face-to-face, on the telephone, or in writing. They express this understanding by working to present themselves in a welcoming manner that supports clear communication and mutual understanding.

Effective communication buoys students to a higher level of achievement and increases the number of parents who are willing to spend their time and energy inside and outside the classroom. In Chapters 2, 3, and 4, we look at the three key ways to communicate invitations to engage in the learning community: sending the message to students and parents that their engagement is not only wanted but necessary; making inroads with resisters by showing them how to go about engaging; and responding positively and effectively to initial refusals.

Sending the Pro-Engagement Message

Words are not the end of thought, they are where it begins.

✽ JANE HIRSHFIELD ✽

Engagement—student and parent—involves that magic time when a person is living in the moment of the activity. Maybe the student is realizing how "kuh," "ah," and "tuh" combine to make the word *cat;* maybe a parent volunteer is realizing that his high-fives during a Field Day challenge run are helping the slowest runners cross the finish line. These are the moments when students and parents feel most part of the school community.

The teacher's role is to send the message to students and parents that these moments are crucial to student learning and to reinforce this idea by implementing regular and varied communication strategies and developing strong interpersonal relationships with parents and students.

In this chapter, we'll look at strategic responses to the following questions:

1. What practices will help you communicate to students and parents that their participation is necessary and welcome?

2. What are some techniques that will help you draw in disaffected students and parents?

3. What is one engagement focus that will directly boost student achievement?

4. What are some simple things you can do to make your engagement outreach more effective?

Practices That Communicate Participation Is Welcome

There will always be naturally gregarious students and parents who respond to learning activities and volunteer opportunities. The others need to be shown that you really do want their participation, and there's a lot you can do, via your words and actions, to open their eyes to this fact and incline them to accept your invitation.

Convincing Students to Engage

Students' willingness to become engaged in the classroom often depends on just a few words. Simply asking one student to "Speak up!" could embarrass her so badly that she will be unable to focus on the lesson for the rest of the class. This student hears your words as criticism and doesn't know how to cope; unlike most adults, she has not learned to distinguish a professional critique of her "work" (here, participation in class discussion) from a personal attack. And so, she responds emotionally and shuts down. This is also why, when you tell Nate he'd do better on his math test if he studied his math facts, he reacts to your sincere suggestion with anger (because he has studied but struggles with memorization) or with sadness (because he has given up hope of ever doing well in math). When it comes to student engagement efforts, never forget how much your words matter.

▶ Give students tools that will help them overcome their fears

Calling students' attention to how their feelings can influence their behavior can imbue them with a sense of power and confidence—and make them more willing to risk classroom participation. Think of teaching them to be aware of their emotional responses as the affective equivalent of metacognition.

For example, you can teach students to analyze their "fight or flight" responses to an uncomfortable situation. "Fight," within the school context, includes name-calling, getting physical, talking back, or bullying. The underlying emotion is a need to defend or speak up for oneself. Once students have grasped how "fight" presents in the classroom, they can work on new and positive ways to express their feelings, including coming up with logical arguments when a classmate disagrees, meeting with the teacher after class for guidance on where work went wrong, and being friendly to classmates instead of threatening.

"Flight" responses involve holding a grudge, becoming upset, or disengaging altogether. They are an indication that the student recognizes that his or her behavior is unacceptable or falling short. The upside of this is an awareness of the need for change. Positive alternative responses can be built on self-analysis: "Why did the other kids call me a tattletale?" "Why did I get a bad grade?" "What can I do differently next time?" Once the student can answer these questions, he or she can formulate different ways to react.

▶ Model and practice behavioral change

It's not enough to simply hope that disengaged students will decide to change their behavior. We have to continually help students understand *why* change would be beneficial and give them guidance on how to plan and execute that change. Here are a few techniques to try:

• *Freeze Frame.* When a student makes a negative comment in the classroom, say, "Freeze frame," and ask the students to restate and evaluate the negative comment. Prompt them to offer alternative responses, out loud or in writing, and then discuss how the new responses differ from the original reaction.

• *Snap Judgment.* Use an overhead projector to show a collection of optical illusions and ask prompting questions to highlight the trick that is being played on their eyes. Al Seckel's books, including *Optical Illusions: The Science of Visual Perception* (2009) and *Super-Visions* (2005), are a great resource. Discuss the confusion students may initially feel when they try to analyze an optical illusion, and draw a connection to the confusion they feel when they are learning something for the first time or are involved in a new personal interaction. Talk about how body language can bring about confusion. For example, a teacher's raised eyebrow might be interpreted as anger, when it is really a thoughtful expression. Pick apart any of these "disconnects" and talk about ways to reconnect.

• *Say What?* Go over some of the common phrases that you use in the classroom and have the students comment on how those phrases affect them: "When the teacher says _____, I think _____. It makes we want to _____." You might learn that saying, "Go spit out your gum" irritates your students and makes them want to chew gum even more! Prompt your students to suggest different ways they would like you to respond to their behavior.

▶ Clarify expectations

All students benefit from knowing where you draw the line for both acceptable behavior and academic achievement, but clear guidelines can be especially beneficial for disengaged students who need the secure structure that guidelines provide. Again, students who feel comfortable in a classroom are more likely to "risk" engagement.

Beyond sharing overall classroom rules and behavioral consequences with my students, I like to distribute behavioral guidelines in Likert-style inventories for students to complete. One such assignment might ask students to rank themselves on a scale of 1 to 5 on different behaviors, such as performing their assigned roles during group work, staying on task, and understanding the assignment's purpose.

When it comes to academic standards, I recommend posting your grading system in the classroom—in a large font and in multiple places. I provide students with a detailed explanation of the system at the beginning of the year. When I do this, I post the sample grade book from Figure 2.1 and introduce some composite students:

1. "Genius Jenae," who aced the quizzes and tests but didn't complete much homework.

2. "Steady Eddie," who completed every assignment and participated in class.

3. "Absent Alva," who didn't participate much in class but completed most assignments and passed most tests.

4. "Inconsistent Ian," who aced every test and participated in class but did not make up missed quizzes or turn in homework.

5. "Superstar Stephen," who performed well in every area.

Figure 2.1
Typical Patterns of Student Achievement

Student	Homework (15% of grade)	Quizzes (25% of grade)	Tests (45% of grade)	Class Participation (15% of grade)	Final Grade
Jenae	35%	96%	95%	85%	85% (B)
Eddie	100%	87%	80%	95%	87t% (B+)
Alva	85%	77%	83%	25%	74% (C)
Ian	20%	67%	98%	25%	68% (D+)
Stephen	100%	95%	96%	100%	98% (A+)

I then ask the students what they see in these sample students. They notice that Steady Eddie actually ended up with a higher average than Genius Jenae. They also notice that the only person who received an *A* was Superstar Stephen, who put the effort into each area. The correlation of effort and achievement may be obvious to adults, but the connection needs to be made explicit to many students.

After the first quarter, consider having one-on-one meetings with students to discuss what they might do to improve their classroom performance. This shows that you care and provides the stimulus students might need to put in that extra effort. I hold such meetings myself, calling each student to my desk one at a time to go over their grades. I point out the elements they performed well on and ask them to deduce where they might apply more effort. Students who tell me, "Wow! I really need to turn in my homework," almost always earn a higher grade for homework the next quarter.

Persuading Parents to Engage

All parents want what is best for their children, but they don't always know the questions to ask or how to get started. Consistent outreach will reinforce that message that engaging in their child's academic life will help their child achieve, and that you are ready and willing to help them find ways to do that. Note that researchers Deslandes and Bertrand (2005) found that parents are more likely to involve themselves in their child's schoolwork, both at home and at school, if they believe teachers and students expect or desire that involvement.

▶ Consider a variety of communication media

Using a wide range of invitation formats can increase your chances that parents will accept your invitation. Traditional methods of communication, such as sending letters home, posting messages on classroom bulletin boards, writing announcements in the school newsletter, and asking students to verbally invite their parents are good starting points.

In addition, you can enlist the help of your parent-teacher organization by asking them to fund business cards that include contact information for each teacher and the school's main office. Pairing this business card with an information sheet for parents to fill out and return (see Figure 2.2) at the beginning of the year will open up an avenue of communication with parents, in the format they prefer, to be used when issues arise with individual students. When you acknowledge their communication format preferences, parents are even more likely to accept your invitation to become engaged.

▶ Strive for clarity

When reaching out to parents, avoid educational jargon or other words that are difficult to understand. In conversation with our colleagues, we might use terms like "differentiated instruction" or "math triads," but parents are more likely to understand what

Figure 2.2
Sample Parent Information Sheet

Talk to Me

To help me communicate with you effectively, please indicate the best way to share information, filling in contact data where appropriate.

When I need to talk to you about your child, I should contact you using:

Home phone	☐ Mom:	☐ Dad:
Work phone	☐ Mom:	☐ Dad:
Mobile phone	☐ Mom:	☐ Dad:
E-mail address	☐ Mom:	☐ Dad:
Letter home	☐ Mom:	☐ Dad:

When I need to share class news:

Text message	☐ Mom:	☐ Dad:
E-mail message	☐ Mom:	☐ Dad:
Class website	☐ Mom	☐ Dad
Class newsletter	☐ Mom	☐ Dad
Class bulletin board	☐ Mom	☐ Dad

you are talking about when you say, "I teach to the individual needs of my students," or "In math, I use a method that encourages students to discuss, examine, and analyze their understanding with me and other students." Writing and speaking in plain, simple language allows your message to be more readily understood.

▶ Create communication routines

Setting up a few standard ways of sharing information with parents and using them on a regular basis is a great way to establish a parental expectation for communication.

There are a couple of approaches I've found very helpful. The first is setting up a two-way method of exchanging reports on student progress and school activities by including a tear-off section at the bottom of every newsletter. To send back questions, request more information, or set up a conference, a parent would just tear off that slip and send it back. The second method is to send different kinds of communications on a certain day of the week— "Take-Home Tuesday" or "Information Friday"—for students to bring home newsletters and announcements. Here, you might use different-colored paper for different purposes, making it easy for parents to spot the green newsletters and blue field trip information flyers among the pile of their child's schoolwork. Sending specific information on predetermined days of the week helps to ensure parents aren't overwhelmed by too much information delivered one piece at a time. This strategy is effective with e-mail as well. After three or four weeks, parents will begin to look for information on that day and seek it out when their child doesn't come home with it or when there's no school communication waiting in their inbox.

Techniques to Entice Disaffected Students and Parents

There are many reasons students and parents might ignore your invitations for engagement. For example, they might have been embarrassed in the past and don't want to repeat that uncomfortable feeling. Implementing some of the following ideas can convince both students and parents that they are safe participating in your classroom.

Flipping Students' Switches from "No" to "Yes"

Students who say no to your requests for attention, hard work, participation, or good behavior are demanding a response from you. It's not comfortable, and it's not easy, but you must cultivate a response that reflects your values and that you are prepared to deliver on a consistent basis. We can't all use humor, and we can't all be drill sergeants, but we can all have high expectations, uphold them consistently, and insist that our students meet them. In doing so, we tell our students that they have the ability to succeed.

▶ Don't "save" students from frustration

Some of the best learning occurs when frustration has set in. Something about working through frustration can forge understanding in a way that is more meaningful than simply listening to someone explain a lesson. It is the bridging of the gap between what is known and what is unknown that will give students the spark of understanding for that one lesson and the desire to create the same spark in future lessons. Creating challenging opportunities for your students that push them to a tolerable level of frustration helps them find personal power in learning—a feeling they will crave once they experience it a few times. Focus on helping your students break problems into parts, locate the resources they need, and figure out a solutions.

Practical Techniques to Help Students
Cope with Classroom Frustration

• *Use physical engagement to get students out of their heads and into the lesson.* Try tossing a tennis ball to the student answering a question during a discussion, and have that student toss the ball back to you after speaking or to another student who wants to continue the response. This kind of activity engages both kinesthetic learners and attention seekers while providing a challenge to introverted students.

• *Teach students appropriate responses to anxiety.* This technique can be as simple as explaining that breathing in slowly through the nose and out through the mouth can return a racing heartbeat to a normal rate and deliberately and specifically creating physical tension and then relaxing (e.g., by intentionally making a fist and squeezing hard for five seconds before releasing) can help reduce tension overall.

• *Discuss the power of positive thinking.* Talk to students about how thoughts influence the outcome of actions. Share the power of changing "I'm going to fail" to "I'll do my best" or "I'm gonna ace this!" You might also discuss choosing a personal motivational phrase or mantra they can repeat to help deal with a challenge, such as "Let's do this!" or "Let's roll!"

▶ Give students the chance to succeed

Even though all schools are designed to promote student success, some students don't perceive their school in this way. Each of our students needs to experience success at school in some manner to ensure they don't give up entirely. They don't have to earn straight As or the highest test scores, but they do need to experience moments where they know that their hard work has paid off. You can foster such success by getting to know your students and encouraging them to share with the classroom—despite any reluctance they may display—so that you can work with them in ways that will help them succeed. The strategies I suggest involve the entire class, not just one or two disengaged students, which facilitates the creation of a classroom community and counteracts the role of some students as "outsiders."

▶ Incorporate opportunities for thinking into your instructional plans

Structured, systemic promotion of reflection and discussion helps build both students' cognitive and metacognitive skills and increases their willingness to express themselves and get involved.

Activities That Stress Thinking

• *Small-group to large-group discussion.* Begin discussions in small groups of two or three students, and then bring the class back together again for a whole-class discussion. The opportunity to speak and be heard in the smaller group builds student confidence and encourages more widespread participation in the whole-class conversation.

• *Brainstorming.* To get the most out of this practice, be careful not to discuss or judge student input as you collect it. Once you've written student ideas on the board, solicit input on which ideas they want to elaborate on or discuss. This way, you're not singling out just one idea to leave behind; instead, you're fostering widespread—and thereby less self-conscious—participation.

• *Active listening.* Assign each student a partner, pairing up students with opposing views on a topic. Give the students a time limit for responding. For the first half of the time period, one student listens and the other student speaks. The listener may not speak unless the speaker gets off topic. Students switch roles for the second half of the time period. When time is up, ask students to create a chart indentifying where their opinions are the same and where they differ. This activity sends the message that different ideas—and the practice of considerate, thoughtful listening—are necessary to encourage productive discussion.

▶ Teach sharing through targeted activities

Instead of putting your students on the spot for their opinion on a discussion, give them options for sharing that allow them to express their opinion in a manner that is comfortable for them.

Activities That Promote Sharing

• *Lineup.* This is a safe way for students to express their opinion on a controversial topic. Ask students to stand in a line representing a continuum of views on the topic, with their place in the line reflecting where they fall on that continuum. Give students opportunities to discuss their views with the students on either side of them to see if they are in the right place. This exercise is twofold, as it gives students a comfortable way to express their opinions and encourages them to take a position and craft their response to an argument, just as they would do when they are involved in a debate or writing a persuasive essay.

• *Categorizing.* Give students the opportunity to group objects or ideas according to criteria that you set; it's a way to help students see patterns and connections and effectively manage new information. In elementary grades, students can categorize objects by size and shape. In middle and high school grades, students can categorize ideas and information chronologically, by how they intersect, or by how they relate to what students already know. This technique can help students integrate new ideas into their knowledge base by giving them concrete steps to follow as they put new ideas into a specific category.

• *Theme in a Bag.* Put items that relate to the theme of your lesson into a bag and ask groups of students to remove one item and prepare an explanation of why that item was in the bag. For a discussion on World War II, you could use an illustration of Uncle Sam, the Star of David, dog tags, a toy paratrooper, a submarine, a map of Pearl Harbor, and a picture of Rosie the Riveter. These objects serve as visual and tactile clues that will foster discussion of key themes that students might otherwise overlook.

Flipping Parents' Switches from "No" to "Yes"

Communicating regularly and effectively serves to stave off interactions that have the potential to derail your efforts to both teach students and engage parents. Create a toolkit of communication methods to provide information, support, and invitations to parents in an effort to send a consistent message that with their help, every child will learn. Both traditional and newer communication methods should be part of your toolkit. But even with improved communication, you may find that some parents go through the motions of school involvement but don't project the sense that they belong in the community. The following strategies will help you welcome even the most distant parent into the fold.

▶ Send out newsletters and make them count

Newsletters (electronic or printed) can be used to connect classroom experience with home experience. Along with assignment due dates, field trip information, and upcoming project details, newsletters can relay specific actions parents can take at home to directly influence their child's performance at school. The newsletter can also include questions for parents to ask their child related to topics the class is studying. Such questions not only provide parents with a bridge to the children's school life but also give students an opportunity to demonstrate leadership by explaining the answers to their parents, who might not be as familiar with the topic.

▶ Embrace the proactive, positive phone call

Too often, when teachers call a student's home, it's because the student is in trouble. But phone calls can do so much more than relay negative information. Regular phone calls to your students' homes are another powerful invitation to parent involvement. They can serve as a means of introducing yourself to parents at the beginning of the school year or as a way of welcoming new families who join the school community midyear. In addition, phoning home about good behavioral choices or academic achievement lets parents see that you are wearing the same team colors they are.

Set a goal of calling three parents each week with positive messages and invitations for involvement. This system will ensure that you will call each child's parents at least a few times during the school year. The phone calls will help you gain an understanding of what the parents perceive as their role in their child's education and provide opportunities for you to listen for clues as to how to increase parent involvement. These conversations are chances for parents to let you know what they need from you. They may not specifically say, "I need help," but if you listen closely, you will know how to respond appropriately. Here are a few examples of parent phone calls that have given me opportunities to provide assistance:

• *When I praised a student's talents* (e.g., "Elena is a natural leader in group projects"), the parents wondered how they might further that ability at home. I was then able to

    ✳ Suggest age-appropriate home responsibilities.

    ✳ Advocate for participation in Girl Scouts, pet walking, or tutoring younger children.

• *When I expressed a concern about academic achievement* (e.g., "Connor is struggling with reading at grade level, and this is slowing down his content comprehension"), the parents admitted that reading had always been hard for them, too. I was then able to

    ✳ Offer a list of outside resources that could help both the parents and the child.

    ✳ E-mail a list of extension exercises that the parent and child could complete together to improve their reading skills.

    ✳ Inquire about scheduling one-on-one tutoring time with the student before or after school hours.

• *When I invited parents to a school event or to volunteer* (e.g., "You are always welcome to eat lunch with Sarah"), the parents told me that their work schedules made visits during the school day impossible. I was then able to

    ✳ Suggest other times that the parents could be present on campus, such as volunteering for campus clean-up on Saturdays, serving as a greeter at the beginning of the school day, or organizing the parent workroom whenever it suited their schedule.

* Assure the parents that their involvement at home is valuable and suggest activities that they and their child could complete together.

* Keep their availability in mind when I send out conference schedules to ensure that they would be able to attend.

▶ Use your class website as a window into your classroom

A class website offers parents an anonymous peek into their children's school world. It's a space where you can share essential information about homework, needed classroom supplies, and upcoming events. In addition, you can create and regularly update a "Helping Your Child Learn at Home" section that provides parents with simple activities that will make a difference in how their child learns.

▶ Use student assignment books for targeted communication

Student planners are great for helping students keep track of homework assignments, but they can also be used as a space for teachers to write personal notes to parents and for parents to ask questions and make requests of teachers. Sending a note home is usually reserved for testing results or behavior issues, but the casual nature of jotting a line in an assignment book makes it an easy and welcoming way to communicate with parents. A teacher could send home the following: "Michael's eyes lit up when we discussed constellations! He said you taught him everything he knows. Would you like to come in and have a sharing session with the class?" This might just be enough of an invitation to encourage a parent to become more engaged in his or her child's academic life, enrich the entire class, and support your curricular goals.

▶ Send reminders via text message and e-mail

With the busy schedule of many parents today, sending reminder invitations via text messages and e-mail increases the chance that parents will attend an upcoming open house, help on testing day, or provide goods for a bake sale.

▶ Hold volunteer days

Giving parents the chance to see what goes on during the school day—and take part in it, too—can be a great way to forge home-school connections. Partner with other teachers and your school's administration to develop volunteer days where parents can drop in throughout an assigned day and complete pre-organized in-school projects for teachers. In this scenario, teachers who need simple projects completed write up directions and then provide all the necessary items (e.g., glue, tape, and scissors) that a parent will need to complete the project, which can range from "crafty" (making alphabet lacing cards for the kindergarten class) to non-crafty (putting together lab packets for older kids' science lessons).

Make sure that there is plenty of direction for your volunteers so that they feel supported in their efforts. You may also want to provide child care for parents with preschool-age students. Volunteer days give parents the chance to see the kind of work teachers put in every day and to contribute their support directly.

▶ Conduct home visits

Visiting reluctant parents in their own environment can create goodwill between school and home and help you begin a relationship with a student's family. In a home visit, you have the time to get to know a family as you listen to their concerns and observe their interactions. Hearing how a parent speaks to her son when she instructs or corrects him can inform your own instructional and classroom management choices. Interacting with the child in a manner similar to his mother's can help a child relax in the school environment and boost his chances of success.

Some topics to consider discussing during a home visit include homework routines, how to set workspace aside for homework, and various home activities that might boost parent-child communication, such as discussing television programs and school activities. You might also suggest other simple things parents can do to boost their child's academic achievement, such as making and using flash cards, listening to and reading along with recorded books at home or in the car, or planning activities during holiday and summer breaks that will help the child maintain basic skills.

Westat and Policy Studies Associates (2001) found involvement practices had a significant and positive effect on student achievement. In schools where teachers reported having high levels of outreach to parents (e.g., meeting face to face with parents, sending parents materials on how to help their child at home, and telephoning routinely), test scores grew at a 40 percent higher rate than in schools where teachers reported low levels of outreach.

We all want higher test scores for our students, and advocating for parent engagement is a clear-cut way to make that happen.

One Engagement Focus That Will Directly Boost Student Achievement

Reading is the key to learning, and all students can benefit from classroom and parent-supported activities that focus on boosting their willingness to read and their enjoyment of reading.

Promoting Student Reading

Students of all ages, and especially struggling readers, need to connect with what they're reading before they can learn from it. Support this connection by offering a broad range of reading materials. When you show your students that reading is important and that you are there to help them when they struggle, they are more inclined to accept your invitation to read. When you involve parents in reading-boosting activities, you double the strength of your message, as students hear it from both you and their parents.

▶ Make books available

The easier it is for students to access books, the more likely they are to read. Students need to be aware of the variety of materials available at the school library, the local library, and online. Once, when our school library was closed due to renovations, I brought a selection of 60 books from the public library into our classroom covering a wide range of subject areas related to our novel study of *A Farewell to Arms*. As the students began to read the books, researching thesis statements for their papers, I heard "I never knew there were books like this in the library!" and "This one is exactly what I needed, Ms. Ridnouer." The papers that I received as a result of this assignment were phenomenal, with cohesive, convincing, and well-supported arguments. We as education professionals must work to remove barriers and build scaffolds to expose students to the interesting and useful aspects of reading. Whenever I hear students lament that reading is boring or fellow teachers complaining that their students won't read, I remember this lesson.

▶ Create interest- and skill-related book lists

Independent reading is encouraged by a marriage of interest and appropriate reading level. Students who are reading about something that appeals to them are willing to work a little bit to understand the material. The more often that connection happens, the more likely they will continue to read on their own. Therefore, one way to encourage reading is to create lists of books arranged by topic and reading level to appeal to your students. Topics for these lists could include sports, music, fashion, performing arts, décor, politics, religion—things that interest students because they are a means of expressing individuality. The website http://librarybooklists.org, which lists and reviews children's and young adult books on a variety of topics, is a great tool for finding high-interest books for your students.

Involving Parents as Reading Advocates

Independent reading is a lifelong skill that has a huge effect on success during the school years. Students who choose to read expose themselves to new ideas and abstract concepts that further their readiness for formal classroom lessons and cultivate their understanding of a broad range of topics. Involving parents in reading intervention and giving them tools to encourage independent reading at home is an effective way to promote this very valuable end (Miedel & Reynolds, 1999). There are a number of practices I can recommend.

▶ Suggest ways for students and parents read together

Offer parents ideas for how to complete partner reading assignments with their children. Some examples follow:

• *Role reading.* One partner reads the character's words with a focus on "sounding" like the character. The other partner reads the narrator's words in a voice that focuses on clearly articulating each syllable.

• *Expressive reading.* One partner reads a paragraph and focuses on using appropriate facial expressions for the character. The other partner reads the paragraph with a focus on changing intonation to suit the characters and their situation.

• *Taking turns.* One partner reads a predetermined amount of text, such as a sentence, paragraph, or page. The other reads the next predetermined amount of text.

Providing parents with lists of discussion questions keyed to assigned texts is a good way to ensure that they know what you're hoping students will gain from the reading.

▶ Provide individualized recommendations

When it comes to recommending texts for parents to read with their child, use what you have learned about the individual student. If you are an elementary teacher, you might want to explore Jim Trelease's *Hey! Listen to This* (1992), which offers read-aloud stories that will entice the reluctant reader. These are grouped by subject and level of difficulty, enabling you to find the perfect story to give parents to read aloud with their children. Trelease's *Read All About*

It! (1993) is a good source for secondary school teachers. It offers writing from various media, including newspaper columns, autobiographical sketches, acclaimed fiction, and feature articles, that covers a wide range of interests such as sports, animals, history, fantasy, and popular culture.

Simple Things That Will Make Your Outreach More Effective

When phone calls, notes, and e-mail exchanges with parents don't succeed in improving a student's performance, you and the parents are bound to become frustrated. It may seem that everyone is working toward improvement except the student. A natural response for parents is to dive in and take over the control of the student's academic life. They might micromanage homework assignments or advocate for the creation of responsibility contracts. Research suggests, however, that too much parental support deprives children of the opportunity to learn from mistakes. In fact, Lee (1994) found a correlation between frequent parent phone calls, conferences, and other communication from parents and students' academic and behavior problems. There are measures you can take to help ensure parent communication will help resolve problems rather than lead to additional ones.

Keeping the Focus on Student Output

There are numerous reasons that students continue to fail in spite of intervention from teachers and parental collaboration. Sometimes students respond poorly to negative attention. Other times, they expect that the adults in their life will "fix" problems when they occur; it doesn't always register with these students that they themselves should be working on the problems at the same time as the adults. And then there are some students who are willing to accept the label of incompetence and carry on with their lives. How can we counteract situations like these and inspire students to make changes to their own performance?

▶ Give students a reason to improve

Some students like to be in charge, even if what they are in charge of is failure. These are the kids who will not improve their handwriting or study their math facts unless they can see a clear reason for doing so. It's a matter of showing them, not telling them. Reflecting on the personalities, social connections, and priorities of these students can help you find an effective approach. For example, you might encourage a student who is disinclined to improve her handwriting to give a special presentation on her favorite topic and write an invitation to her classmates. Peer pressure and the personal importance of the message will encourage her to write neatly. Similarly, you might invite a bright student who refuses to study his math facts to come in for lunchtime math challenges that ratchet upward in difficulty as his speed and accuracy improve.

▶ Encourage personal and academic self-expression

Allowing students to be creative and represent themselves in their work promotes the feeling that they are understood, which can increase individual motivation. One way to do this to ask all students to create a visual presentation about themselves for the class's online newsletter. Such presentations give me all kinds of insight into my students' talents and inspirations—what they love, what they are willing to fight for, and where they see themselves going.

I also recommend routinely giving students the opportunity to explain how they understand course content and to articulate how they see things. Remember that one student might memorize his math facts by recalling that "Five times 9 is 45," while another one might visualize five rows of nine blocks—each way is valid. As students build awareness of the way they learn, they will default to their learning style more frequently and process new ideas more quickly.

Fine-Tuning Parent Communication

You will find that you have parents who say they aren't able to become involved and parents who want to be in your classroom every day. It is your job as the classroom teacher to create boundaries that encourage the "underinvolved" parents and provide structure to manage potentially "overinvolved" ones.

▶ Be clear with volunteers

Focus requests for parent involvement on a concrete activity to guide parents' efforts toward activities that utilize their skill sets and maximize the time they have available. Ask parents when they are available to volunteer and what types of activities they are interested in helping with. Generate a list of simple volunteer activities and post it in the classroom, in your class newsletter, and on your website. Following are some ideas for your list:

Volunteer Opportunities at School

• Assist and supervise students in learning centers, reading and math groups, and daily jobs

• Work with students requiring assistance with a specific need (e.g., math facts, spelling, comprehension, oral reading)

• Help students with in-class writing

• Organize class parties and plays

• Organize student work

• Make copies, check daily work, file items, and prepare crafts

• Put up bulletin boards

• Assist students with backpacks, school supplies, and coats

• Serve as a school tour guide

• Offer assistance in the parent resource room, school office, cafeteria, or library

• Serve as a hall monitor before or after school

• Publish student books

• Lead an after-school activity, such as art, crafts, gardening, or chess

Volunteer Activities at Home

- Cut out student activity pieces
- Cut out laminated items
- Create a school brochure or school information magnet
- Collate and staple exams
- Make board games, flash cards, and manipulatives
- Type up book orders
- Update the class website
- Design (or redesign) the class newsletter
- Contribute content for the class newsletter and website
- Translate classroom communication for nonnative speakers

▶ Match parent activity to parent interest

Parents will appreciate being able to pick an activity that suits their interests and schedules. In addition, they will be proud to be able to contribute to the classroom environment in a meaningful way. As a parent, when I was given the opportunity to help a teacher achieve a goal for her students that she wasn't able to do on her own—leading a six-week writing workshop that culminated in a bound book of student work—I was proud to share my skills and even more inclined to volunteer in the future.

When parents have completed a volunteer activity, ask them to respond to a feedback form like the one in Figure 2.3 to give them a chance to evaluate their experience and provide you with information about how their efforts benefited the students. As you read the volunteer evaluations, assess the productivity of the parents' involvement with the students and their overall satisfaction with the activity. Parents who judge themselves as ineffective in one task could be offered another type of volunteer opportunity that is better suited to their skill set, or reassured that they were indeed effective. This evaluation form encourages the idea that even if one volunteer effort doesn't go smoothly, volunteering is still a worthwhile exercise.

Figure 2.3
Sample Volunteer Feedback Form

═══

Volunteer Feedback Form

Please provide feedback about your volunteer efforts to help me ensure that your experience was valuable to both you and the students.

Describe your volunteer activity:

What changes would you recommend to the volunteer activity?

What aspects of your volunteer experience gave you a sense of satisfaction?

What aspects gave you feelings of frustration?

Is there another volunteer activity you would prefer?　　　☐ Yes　　☐ No

If you choose "Yes," please describe the volunteer activity you are interested in:

How would you rate the productiveness of your involvement with the students?

☐ Highly productive　　　　　☐ Moderately productive

☐ Productive　　　　　　　　☐ Unproductive

Communication Is the Beginning of Engagement

Maintaining effective communication with students and parents opens the door to engagement. As you present varied avenues for the discovery, cultivation, and expression of ideas, you help students and parents alike see idea creation as something they want to pursue and school as a space where their contributions are valued. Encourage students and parents to view the school and classroom as an open community, and help them find their place within it.

Making Inroads
with Resisters

The art of teaching is the art of assisting discovery.

✳ MARK VAN DOREN ✳

You know that buzz that you get when your students understand a lesson and can't wait to learn more? It's one of the things that infuses joy into the job of teaching. However, it's likely you also know the hurdle that gets in the way of those great, "buzzy" moments: those few students who consistently do not understand the lesson and are unwilling to stretch themselves to reach for that understanding. These students communicate their resistance to engagement in myriad ways. A high school student might stop doing classwork or homework altogether. An elementary student might feign sickness, and a middle school student might skip class. Sometimes students just check out mentally, relying on their mere physical presence to carry them through the day's requirements. Having students decline your invitation to become engaged in the classroom can be quite a buzz kill.

Parents can also decline invitations for engagement. Some might thank you for all your work but say, "I'm just too busy." Some might not respond to you at all. Others might silently believe that school is the teacher's world, home is their world, and never the twain shall meet. Don't be discouraged. You know better. You know that students and parents enter into engagement more readily when they understand how their involvement helps every child succeed.

Of course, if it were easy to get students and parents engaged, we'd all be doing it already. These skills are not usually taught to teachers in training but rather deduced by experienced teachers over time. This chapter offers tools to help you more effectively advocate engagement to those students and parents who consistently resist these invitations. Here are the questions this chapter will address:

1. How do you encourage students and parents to be coteachers?

2. What is one simple thing that will promote better communication?

3. What are the best ways to promote homework completion?

4. What are some achievement-boosting activities to try?

How to Encourage Students and Parents to Become Coteachers

A "coteacher" is anyone who takes an active role in the instructional process. It can be a student, engaging actively in his or her own instruction and learning, or it can be parent, engaging actively in the instruction focused on his or her child.

I have found that it's possible to lure students who say "no" to learning back into it by calling their attention to the small decisions that they make every day—choices that can either add to or detract from their education. Bringing about this kind of awareness encourages and enables them to choose to be engaged and helps them become more self-directed as learners.

Parent-teacher conferences, during which you share a student's grades and progress and talk over his or her achievements, struggles, social interactions, and interests are the ideal forum for enlisting parents as coteachers. One point I like to share with parents is the value of helping their children define themselves as "students." As Epstein (2001) notes, "If youngsters do not define themselves as 'students' then they must be something else, with no need to be in school. Those who feel the support of their family, teachers, peers, and community for their work as students are more likely to maintain that view of themselves and stay in school" (p. 62). Getting parents to view their children as students, to *call* their children "students," and to support their children's academic efforts can help improve academic achievement across the board.

Aligning Student Interests with Curricular Goals

Engaging students in learning activities that pique their interests and nudge their skill level toward proficiency doesn't just help them complete tasks in the classroom; it also helps them develop coping mechanisms for when they feel disconnected or bored. Boredom blocks learning, and all too many teachers know how difficult it can be to break through the "wall of boredom" once the first few bricks have been laid.

▶ Work with student preferences

Students in the 21st century are involved in all types of activities that are relatively new to our culture, such as texting, instant messaging, multiplayer online video games, and watching reality TV shows. These activities highlight personal choice, which a teacher can extend through peer-to-peer interaction, such as discussion, debate, and group projects where they are able to create presentations, role-play, and engage in art and drama activities. By contrast, teacher lecture, the primary instructional method of my generation (and probably yours as well), is seen by today's students as the least effective path to engagement (Yazzie-Mintz, 2006). Here are some ideas for hands-on lessons designed to engage by building on student preferences.

• *Social studies.* Ask students to compose an instant message (IM) interview with Thomas Jefferson as a prewriting exercise for an essay. Have students swap IMs via e-mail and rewrite the truncated messages into standard English, adding questions and comments to solicit more information. This exercise allows students to work in a format they are comfortable with, and they are likely to feel freer to offer constructive criticism to their peers because they are typing instead of expressing it aloud.

• *Algebra.* Ask students to design a MySpace or Facebook page for Pi. Consider discussion questions such as the following: Who would Pi "friend"? Whose friend requests would Pi ignore? What details would be in Pi's profile? What would be posted on Pi's wall? What kinds of pictures would Pi post? All of these elements could be considered as part of the student's grade. The more algebra concepts incorporated into the page, the higher the grade. This exercise shows students that their teacher respects an activity they value, and in return, the students will integrate the teacher's new ideas more readily into their understanding.

Using Parent-Teacher Conferences to Share Insider Information

Everyone likes to be an insider—someone "in the know." Play on this human trait during your annual parent-teacher conferences. Because every parent has an inherent interest in attending their child's conference, this is a unique opportunity to invite input from parents and help them feel comfortable working with you. This comfort can prove to be a base from which parent engagement can flourish.

Most teachers feel unprepared to conduct effective parent conferences when they begin teaching. But most of us also agree that conferences can be the best opportunity for teachers and parents to discuss each other's perspectives on a student and to develop a plan that will serve the student's needs. In addition, conferences give you the chance to have a conversation with parents that helps them envision roles for themselves within the classroom community.

▶ Invite students to attend parent-teacher conferences

Inviting students to be active participants in conferences serves as a reminder of the purpose of the meeting—to help this particular student achieve in school. Having the student present also sends a strong message to students that these people are gathered to help. It tells them that they are worth their teacher's and their parents' time—an invaluable message. Christenson and Sheridan (2001) report that students benefit from seeing "significant adults working together to help, hearing adults share their expectations of students, contributing solutions that increase their investment in the outcome, and witnessing processes and not having to rely on others' interpretations" (p. 192).

▶ Provide talking points

A few days before the conference, provide parents with a list of talking points, like the one shown in Figure 3.1. The questions will help parents put together questions in advance and place them on equal footing, as an active meeting participant. During the meeting itself, use the list as an agenda, supplementing with samples of the student's work and observations about the student. When parents see that you have taken the time and care to collect and manage their child's work, they know that you are focusing your attention on the development of each student.

▶ Don't placate; instigate!

During the conference, don't waste parents' time with bland comments meant to pacify them. While it might be nice to hear "Your daughter's doing great!" and "Your son just needs to keep up the good work," these comments don't provide a clear picture of their child's performance. Sharing that Jane is truly clever and then

Figure 3.1

Talking Points for the Parent-Teacher Conference

• How much time does your child spend on homework most nights?

• How would you describe the type of assistance you offer to your child?
  ☐ My child works without my assistance.
  ☐ I am there to clarify directions.
  ☐ I review my child's work when it is complete and point out errors.
  ☐ I sit with my child and help step by step.

• What are your child's academic strengths and weaknesses?

• What are your child's nonacademic strengths and weaknesses?

• How would you describe your child's social interaction with peers?
  ☐ My child prefers to play alone.
  ☐ My child plays primarily with siblings and relatives.
  ☐ My child has many friends he/she enjoys playing with.
  ☐ My child has a few close friends he/she enjoys playing with.

• Does your child show evidence of giftedness in a specific area?

• What after-school programs has your child participated in?

• Does your child contribute to dinner discussions?

• How would you describe your child's ability to complete a task independently?
  ☐ My child struggles to complete a task alone.
  ☐ My child is capable of managing one- or two-step tasks.
  ☐ My child is capable of managing all tasks.

• What words have you heard your child use to describe his/her school experience?

• What information can I provide to assist you in helping your child?

• When is the best time to contact you?

• What is the best way to reach you?

☐ Home phone: ☐ E-mail:
☐ Mobile phone: ☐ Letter home

offering an example of how clever she is helps Jane's dad visualize his child at school. Offering suggestions on how to build on Nathan's speed with math facts or ideas for how he might improve his skills in punctuation will be far more helpful to Nathan's mom than unspecific praise. Instead of complaining that Helen is an attention-hungry child, suggest to Helen's dad that she take a drama class or a singing class. Recommend that a shy child could help parents in a "Meals on Wheels" program.

Parents want to know that you honor their role in their child's life and that you know their child is much more than a standardized test score. Demonstrate that understanding by listening to the parent describe how gentle their son is with the family's new baby, how their daughter adores soccer, and how their twins both thought *Bridge to Terabithia* was a much better book than a movie. Solicit these stories from parents to validate their role in their child's education and to find common ground in the classroom for the student.

▶ Encourage the reinforcement of social skills

During the conference, stress to parents that they can give their child a leg up in the classroom by focusing on three specific areas at home: reinforcing positive social skills, analyzing social interaction, and coaching emotional responses. Students need lots of reinforcement to develop new classroom habits, which can include nitpicky details such as sitting properly and responding, "Yes, please," to a question. Consider pinpointing a few social skills that your students are struggling with that parents could reinforce at home. Maintaining eye contact, for example, can influence a student's success at school. It's a means of exchanging information and ensuring attention, and it can affect how others perceive you. Figure 3.2 shows an example of a handout enlisting the help of parents in practicing a much-needed skill.

Figure 3.2

Sample Parent Handout:
Promoting Social Skill Development at Home

We're Making Contact!

This month, our classroom is going to work on increasing the amount of eye contact we use with one another. This is an important social skill—and one that will help us build our classroom community and help all students learn better.

Your help at home will make this challenge a success!

For starters

Become part of my teaching team by increasing your use of eye contact and encouraging your child to use eye contact when speaking to you and others.

Suggested activities:

• Practice using eye contact on family walks.
• Discuss difficulties with questions such as the following:

☐ Is making eye contact easy or difficult for you? Why?
☐ What type of information does eye contact give you?
☐ How does eye contact make you feel about the person you are speaking with?

• Ask your child to pass an object to you without using eye contact. When he/she passes the object, say, "Thank you," and don't use eye contact. Then sit down for a quick chat, using the following questions:

☐ "How did you like the way I made my request?"
☐ "How did it make you feel?"
☐ "Would eye contact make you feel differently?"
☐ "How could eye contact help you in the classroom?"

Why I stress this in my classroom

Making eye contact during conversation is a valuable life skill. Scientific research has found that through the use of our eyes, we can control interactions, elicit the attention of others, and show our level of interest in the information being communicated.

Other social skills you might encourage parents to reinforce at home include

- Reading body language, facial expressions, and tone of voice
- Appropriately using the parts of a social interaction, including greetings, starting a conversation, the back and forth of conversation, and listening
- Maintaining appropriate physical distance from others
- Going with the flow of a game
- Recovering from disappointment or anger
- Considering another person's point of view

▶ Stress the importance of emotional interaction

When students experience changes in their emotional state, they often become frustrated because they don't have the life experience to know that such fluctuation is normal. Emotionally balanced people know how to assess which emotion they are feeling, understand that feeling, and understand the feelings of those around them. Becoming a balanced person takes a lot of practice.

During the parent-teacher conference, enlist parents' help in reinforcing the discussions you have in your classroom about managing emotions to help students become more adept at recognizing and responding to their feelings.

Share with parents the common struggles of students in your grade level. This will help to prepare them for the emotional comments they might hear from their children and offer them useful ideas about how to respond. Elementary students might say, "I hate the lunch lady"; middle school students, "The boys are bullies"; high school students, "I can't stand any of the teachers at my school." Suggest that parents use the following steps to respond:

- *Step 1.* Recognize and validate your child's emotion by responding, "You are angry."
- *Step 2.* Create a teachable moment by asking, "How is this person different from other people you know?"

- *Step 3.* Listen to your child's answer, while showing appropriate body language and offering verbal encouragement, such as "Yes, go on."
- *Step 4.* Help your child develop a solution.

One Simple Thing That Promotes Better Communication

Journalist, writer, and teacher Brenda Ueland (1993) once observed, "When we are listened to, it creates us, makes us unfold and expand. Ideas actually begin to grow within us and come to life" (p. 205). This is a wonderful way of expressing the importance of communication with a student. Too often, instead of engaging in dialogue, teachers and parents alike focus on getting information: Did David turn in his homework? Did Sarah remember to study her math facts? Does he have a pencil? Is she on time? Did he do everything I asked? As a teacher and parent myself, I know too well that conversations with young people can easily become less about idea sharing and more about ticking items off of a to-do list. The first step toward promoting communication is to become mindful of your goal and to create strategies that will help you meet it. When your students' parents confess to you that they are frustrated with an incommunicative child, share techniques that will help them meet their child on common ground.

Being an Audience for Each of Your Students

All students benefit from knowing that their teacher cares about them and wants them to do well. It's a personal connection that lays the foundation for more effective communication and more effective instruction. However, in a crowded classroom, and with curriculum standards to address and dozens of benchmarks to meet, giving individual students undivided attention is no easy thing. The following suggestions might help with this process.

▶ Make yourself available—and publicize that availability

One of the best pieces of advice I can offer is to create office hours and stick to them. Advertise that this time is available and make students feel welcome, and they will come.

I post my "office hours" outside my door with appointment slips in a pocket for students to fill out and give me. My students like the official process, which lends a professional tone to our meeting and encourages them to limit the meetings to serious topics. I take their note, write their name on my calendar, and hand the slip back to them. This helps them to remember to show up!

This easy strategy conveys to students that you mean it when you say you would like to talk to them and shows them that you are willing to give them the tools they need to be successful.

▶ Convey to students that you value their concerns

When you invite students to come talk to you, you are saying, "You have something worthwhile to say." The students are more likely to think about what they are going to talk to you about when you make it clear that you will listen to them. Respond to their concerns with questions such as, "What makes you say that?" "How do you see this in your everyday life?" and "I don't know. Why don't you do some research on that and get back to me so we can share it with the class?"

▶ Let students be the authority

When students meet with you voluntarily, let them set their own agenda. Remember, these meetings are about improving communication above anything else, so other behavioral or academic issues can wait. If your issue can't wait, then you ought to call a meeting yourself!

Alerting Parents to Small Changes
That Can Have a Big Impact

Sometimes it is the little things that can prevent effective communication. Give parents insight into small changes they can make in their everyday interactions that will help their children achieve. Help parents communicate with their children by offering a few simple suggestions.

▶ Recommend the banishment of "but"

The word "but" shapes so many conversations—and often not for the better! Suggest to parents that they try an experiment in which they try refraining from saying "but" in the conversations they have with their child. Explain that this is a simple way to keep the focus positive, which will promote conversation, and steer away from negative feelings, which tend to shut down parent-child conversation. Consider the following:

> *Parent:* "An *A* in math is great, Susan, but a *C* in science? How did *that* happen?"

At this point, the *A* in math might as well not even be on the report card. Report card time is an ideal occasion for parents to try this experiment. Send home a list of suggestions for how parents might replace negative "buts" with comments that are positive and will still encourage improvement:

> *Parent:* "An *A* in math! I know you worked hard for that. And I see you're still working at that science grade. Keep at it."

▶ Share conversational tools

So often parents ask their children yes-or-no questions, such as "Can't you see it my way?" "Did you have a good day?" or "Did you follow the directions?" When their children answer "no" to each of these, parents might feel a little frustrated about how to get more information from their children. Help parents communicate effectively with their children by offering them tools to engage their children in meaningful dialogue. Use handouts, newsletter articles, and postings on the class website to share tips for steering conversations in directions that will allow students to practice developing and articulating ideas (see Figure 3.3 for an example of such a handout).

Encouraging parents to incorporate a few of these conversation starters into their daily speech furthers a key educational objective: students' being able to articulate their ideas. It also helps students feel heard, and it's a simple way for you to promote a positive connection between parent and child.

▶ Advocate reading together

Suggest to parents that they cut out a magazine or newspaper article that they and their child can read together. When both have finished the reading, the child can interview the parent about the topic or quiz the parent on specific facts. If it seems like more scaffolding would be welcome, provide scripted questions such as "What was the main topic of the article?" "What did you learn about this topic?" and "What else would you like to know about this topic?" You could also suggest that the parent and child take turns choosing the article or consider topics aligned with the curriculum.

▶ Play up the educational value of fun activities

Christenson and Sheridan (2001) contend that when parents are mindful of the way they speak to their children and consistently involve themselves in positive activities, such as eating meals together, visiting the library, and setting high goals and expectations, scholastic achievement is increased. Assure parents that there is educational value in things they might think of as pure fun: watching movies with their kids, attending sports events as a family, or listening to music together. For children, just being with Mom or Dad is validating. This "together time" connects children to the adult world of school and home, and it also serves as source material for all kinds of parent-child conversations.

▶ Provide simple tips for starting conversations and keeping them going

Here are a few tips I recommend with regularity:

• Capture your child's attention by saying, "You know what I saw today?"

• Show your child you've been paying attention to them by saying, "I really liked when I saw you do/say..."

• Demonstrate that conversation is valuable by sitting down to talk, listening actively, and making eye contact.

• Encourage your child to keep talking by nodding and making comments like "Yes," "I see," and "Go on."

Figure 3.3

Sample Website Post:
Jump-Starting Conversations with Your Child

Parents, remember *you have the opportunity to develop your child's thinking skills every single day.* Initiating conversations jump-starts your child's thought process. Try adding a few of these conversation starters to your daily dialogue with your child. Also watch out for conversation enders.

Conversation Starters	**Conversation Enders**
"I'm listening..."	"I'm the adult here. Do what you're told."
"What do you think?"	"If your friends jumped off a bridge,
"I don't know. Let's Google it."	would you do the same?"
"What else do you know about that?"	"You couldn't possibly understand."
"What do you notice about that?"	"Let me do that for you."
"That's a great question!"	"That is none of your business."
"What does that mean to you?"	"You are too young to know about that!"
"Do you want to talk about it?"	"Why would you want to know about
	such a thing?"
	"That's your problem."

The Best Way to Promote Homework Completion

Homework—specifically the undone and incomplete kind—is a common source of frustration for teachers, students, and parents.

Supplying Rungs for the Homework Ladder

Although students can come up with a long list of excuses for not doing their homework, generally their excuses fall into three categories:

1. They don't feel that the homework is necessary.

2. They don't understand the assignment.

3. They don't have a structure in place that supports good homework habits.

The best way to address the problem of incomplete homework is to address these excuses head on.

▶ Defend your assignments (and make sure they're defensible)

If students claim they don't think homework is necessary, respond with the reasons that it is: Homework gives them a chance to practice skills and apply understandings addressed in class. It helps them build on what they have learned, internalize processes, and connect to the next stage of instruction.

Of course, it's your prerogative to make sure this defense is accurate! When you can, design homework assignments that include a few tasks or problems just like the ones you and the students did together in class, but also include some that put novel, engaging twists on the material. For example, when teaching fractions to 4th graders, you might assign the "problem" of dividing an apple or a slice of bread in to fourths, thirds, eighths, and so on. In a 6th grade social studies class, ask students to demonstrate their understanding of the reading material using a graph, pie chart, or Venn diagram.

▶ **Make homework count**

I believe that homework needs to be graded or otherwise scored, and that students should understand how homework will be weighted in their overall grade. In my experience, if students believe that you're not actually going to review work and give them a score that reflects their effort, they will not invest that effort—producing substandard work and not reaping any reward from the assignments.

I recommend allowing students to turn in homework late—with a point penalty. This policy underscores that it's the substance of homework that's important, and that although there is cost for not following directions, it is a cost they can afford.

▶ **Never give homework assignments as a punishment**

Students who are punished with homework tend to equate future homework assignments with being in trouble or as a weapon in a power struggle they may be engaging in with you, their teacher. Again, it's a case of obscuring or negating the real, helpful purpose of homework.

▶ **Create consistent reminders and expectations**

Post homework assignments in a designated, visible place in your classroom. This practice sends the message that homework is worthy of your time and classroom space, thereby encouraging students to see its value.

▶ **Emphasize skills that support good homework habits**

Direct instruction in how to complete homework successfully will discourage students from saying, "I just can't do it!" and encourage them to say, "I know just how I will get this done!" Focus especially on the following three:

• *Organizational skills*. Give students a choice of not *if* they will be organized, but *how* they will be organized. Bring in some organizer options for them to choose from, ranging from a pocket notebook to an official agenda with a space for each subject each day.

• *Time management skills.* Give students an idea of how long an assignment should take them. Encourage students who take much longer than the time you have suggested to make an appointment to talk about their homework process, so you can help determine what is causing the problem and figure out a solution.

• *Study strategies.* Create a "plan of attack" that students can apply to homework by asking them questions about the process in class and discussing their responses. Here are some sample questions and responses to start you off:

✱ *Do they do homework from their favorite subject first or save it for last?* Encourage students to try both ways and see which way suits them best.

✱ *What do they do if they get confused by a question or aren't sure how to approach a problem?* Let students know that confusion is the gateway to learning. If they can recognize what they feel like when they are confused, they can develop a response that will help them bridge the gap from confusion to understanding.

✱ *What is the best time for them to study?* Ask students if they are morning magpies or night owls, and then suggest ways to capitalize on this tendency.

✱ *How long do they study for at a time?* Encourage students to be mindful of how much time passes before they begin to feel restless during a homework session. It could be 15 minutes, 30 minutes, or an hour. Whatever the case, tell them to recognize their body's signals and use a timer to alert them to the need for study breaks, putting them in charge of their study time.

✱ *What is their study environment like?* Some people study better with music; some people need silence. Some people need order; others can work in chaos. Talk about the impact these and other environmental elements can have on homework comple-tion to help your students understand that homework doesn't just happen. Completing homework takes mindful effort—effort they can control!

Creating Starting Points for Parents

Many parents don't know where to begin with helping their students, and others will certainly appreciate a reminder of how to coax the best results from their children. Providing clear-cut guidelines to parents about how they can effectively assist with homework is a good way to ensure that the children will begin to see themselves as students.

▶ Encourage a mental and physical environment that supports homework

When it comes to homework, one of the best ways parents support their children is by maintaining an environment where homework is a priority. This means emphasizing the value of working hard at the tasks assigned, supervising study habits, and limiting both extracurricular activities and household chores as needed to ensure there is time for homework. These are just a few of the habits that Mordkowitz and Ginsburg (1987) identify as characteristic of parents of successful students. These parents talked with their children about the relationship between effort, schooling, and success in life, and they provided resources—such as rulers, calculators, and workbooks—necessary to support their children's academic efforts. They also raised their children to believe that completing a task is simply a matter of figuring out *how* it will get done; *if* the task will get done is not a consideration. See Figure 3.4 for a sample handout for parents on the topic of homework, incorporating many of the lessons of the Mordkowitz and Ginsburg study.

Achievement-Boosting Activities to Try

So much of student learning depends on the attitude that students bring to the learning experience. Students who feel able to perform well are poised to absorb so much more than those who come in feeling dumb. In this section, I offer some strategies to help students see themselves as capable so that when they become frustrated with a new idea, they have the confidence to push through to understanding.

Figure 3.4
Sample Parent Handout: Helping Your Child with Homework

Some Homework Do's and Don'ts for Parents

DO
• Give your child a well-lit, quiet space that is stocked with pens, pencils, a dictionary, and paper.
• Create a routine around homework.
• Be available for encouragement.
• Communicate with the teacher when your child is not able to complete an assignment.
• Encourage your child by saying things like "You are doing great!" and "Hard work pays off!"
• Talk to your child regularly about what he or she learned from homework assignments.
• Refer to your child as a "student" as often as possible.

DON'T
• Allow your child to complete homework in front of the television.
• Expect your child to figure out when to do homework.
• Give your child the answers when he or she struggles.
• Believe that a problem will sort itself out.
• Cook, clean, or watch television when homework involves you.
• Discourage your child by saying things like "This is taking you too long!" and "It can't be *that* hard!"
• Ignore the opportunity to discuss homework with your child.
• Allow your child to refer to himself/herself as "bad at math" or "a bad reader."

Using Success to Build Success

The times in my life that have made me feel the most successful are moments when I have seen my success in the eyes of somebody that I admire. When somebody else's words or actions reflect an appreciation for an activity that I know I put time and hard work into, I feel successful. Create activities that give your students the chance to experience this feeling, activities that require a deliberate process and achieve a valuable end product. Be constantly mindful of how else you can engage your students by communicating messages that say, "You are capable, and I know this because I have witnessed it before. Let's do this!"

▶ Extend K-W-L

The K-W-L group instruction strategy, credited to Donna Ogle (1986), instructs students to fill out a sheet listing what they *K*now, what they *W*ant to know, and when they have completed the lesson, what they have *L*earned. It is widely used as pre- and post-activity self-assessment for students and teachers to evaluate the learning process. You can extend the use of this vital tool to enrich your personal insight into your students and to help your students feel understood and acknowledged.

At the beginning of the school year, introduce the K-W-L strategy and tell students, "Today, we are not using K-W-L to understand our subject matter. Instead, we are using K-W-L because *you* matter." Hand out individual K-W-L worksheets to the class. In the *K* column, ask students to list those topics and ideas that they have particular knowledge of or interest in. In the *W* column, ask student to list everything they want to learn, no matter the subject. Leave the *L* column blank. Use their *K* and *W* responses to guide you in planning your lessons throughout the year and to help you zero in on effective praise that will motivate your students.

At the end of your time with the students, return the sheets to the students and ask them to fill in the *L* column with what they learned while they were in your class. They will be amazed at what they had written previously, and you will be creating a model for evaluating and understanding future ideas that they want to learn more about.

▶ Respond to student expectations

Some students can roll with whatever happens to them. Others become unsettled when lunch is late or math time bleeds into science time. If a student says, "But you said we were going to the media center at 10:00. It's 10:05. Let's go!" try responding, "Sometimes we can't stick to the schedule perfectly. Help me collect the scissors. We will be leaving soon." Responding calmly and engaging the student in a responsible or positive way models how to deal with the uncertainties of the class environment.

Be mindful of the range of personalities in your classroom, and help anxious students develop tools to reduce their anxiety and help them perform successfully in the classroom. All students will benefit from this type of modeling. For example, begin the class period with a summary of what you and the students will be doing. If you change gears, clearly state why and explain the new assignment: "I had said we were going to discuss Carl Sandburg's poem 'Fog,' but the sun is shining so brightly, let's read 'At a Window' instead."

Encouraging Parents to Make the "Educational Most" of Free Time

Time after school and on weekends offers parents the opportunity to involve their children in activities that will help them perform better academically. Routinely share handouts with parents suggesting developmentally appropriate, home-based activities that will reinforce the curriculum, help students develop necessary foundational skills and background knowledge, and emphasize community connections.

▶ **Design parent-child activities that reinforce the curriculum**

Extra practice is always a good idea. Examples might include the following:

- Create a scavenger hunt for students and their parents to find local flora and fauna, complete with pictures and a description of their appearance during the different seasons.
- Promote parent involvement in practicing estimation skills. Students can be asked to estimate the outside temperature, the number of beans in a jar, how much pasta to cook for dinner, or how many minutes until bedtime.

▶ **Assign homework that develops foundational skills**

Skill-based learning can happen outside the classroom with assignments similar to these:

- Provide an explanation of the different exercises students are learning in their physical education class. Ask parents to complete the exercises with their child or give bonus points for a parent's signature indicating that the parent watched the student complete all the exercises.
- Encourage organizational skills by asking parents to cut newspaper articles into paragraphs. Middle and high school students can put the paragraphs in the correct order. Elementary students can do the same with comic strips.
- Ask parents to assign their child the job of organizing an area of the house, such as the family junk drawer, the laundry, or the child's own sock drawer. When the child is done, they can discuss why organization is important and how this skill relates to organizing class notes, desks, and lockers at school.
- Suggest that parents set aside reading time every night when they read to their children, and then have the children read quietly to themselves.

▶ Encourage parents to develop their child's background knowledge

Promote the idea that students are lifelong learners by creating homework activities that appeals to students' sense of adventure. Here a few ways you might do that:

• Assign a virtual trip to an exotic location. Ask students to research the cost of the trip, including airfare, hotels, and rental cars. Then instruct them to research the highlights of the area, the foods to try, and the different cultural practices. Students can then create dishes from that area and use a few phrases from the area's native tongue during dinner with their families.

• Forge connections between students' homework assignments and their home life by asking them to complete a Connections Journal where they and their parents brainstorm the ways they see homework relating to a life skill.

▶ Take advantage of community connections

Promote the idea that learning happens everywhere. Here are some sample activities to consider:

• Ask parents to take their children to a local historic spot and collect informational brochures to be used in the classroom. The student will gain academic knowledge during the visit that will be reinforced by bringing back educational information for the teacher to use in the classroom.

• Explore opportunities for service learning. High school students can participate in Habitat for Humanity; younger students can sort items for community centers.

• Assign children the task of calculating the pretax total of the items purchased during a trip to the grocery store. Children can use a calculator to add up the items as they go; when they are in line, they can subtract discounts from coupons and in-store deals.

• Initiate parent-child baking sessions by explaining how baking is a practical application of math skills: students learn how to add, use fractions, and learn about temperature. They also learn the practical skills of following a recipe and working with a partner.

• Suggest parents set aside "date" days where the child gets to set the itinerary.

• Recommend putting kids in charge of caring for a particular plant in the house or a section of the family garden.

Intentional Targeting Pays Off

Each day is an opportunity to pass on a positive lesson to your students and their parents—even to the most reticent participants or outright resistors. By consistently looking out for those parents and students who are not engaged and creating new ways to engage them, you are casting a wider and wider net that will eventually catch even those who are the most resistant. Offering tools for partnership in the classroom promotes students as coteachers, facilitating deeper learning. Offering tools to parents to discuss nonacademic issues in depth helps them become coteachers at home, teaching skills and addressing issues that will enhance their children's school experience. Everybody wins.

Regrouping and Rebounding After Rejection

P art of your job is to figure out how to break through walls to student and parent engagement or to build a ladder over those walls. The methods we've discussed so far offer good ways to approach this work. But all teachers will have students and parents whose past school and life experiences make them especially reluctant to engage as learners and as supporters of learning. What do you do when your invitations to engagement do not have the hoped-for result?

I'm all for persistence, but it doesn't make sense to keep inviting participation in the same way, over and over again, when those invitations are repeatedly rejected. Better to refocus on the goal of empowering students and parents and seek new—and more personalized—ways to reach them one by one.

Here are the key questions we'll address:

1. How do you address students' and parents' negative histories?

2. How do you handle conflict without undoing all the work you've done to establish connections?

3. How do you promote the idea that sharing concerns and skills is a good thing that benefits the whole classroom community?

How to Address Students' and Parents' Negative Histories

Students and parents enter your classroom with years of experiences that have shaped them and their engagement choices in both positive and negative ways. The ones with the positive history are usually the ones participating at a high level. Keep in mind the need to focus your attention on those students whose histories include academic failure or social struggle. Do they have poor reading skills? Are they struggling with basic math? Have they had difficulty making friends? Seeking to understand your students remains the best way to form a connection with them.

I've found that parents' histories often have a lot of influence over their willingness to become engaged in their child's education. Typical impediments are factors such as their own academic experiences and social struggles, accompanied by a fear of judgment. These parents need a compassionate approach to engagement—one that stresses they are valuable to the classroom just the way they are. You can reinforce this idea by highlighting and applauding the individual traits of the families in your class and showcasing them for the entire class, or even the entire school, to see.

Examining and Rethinking Student Behaviors

Particular student behaviors are often seen as barriers to learning. In *Blessings of a Skinned Knee,* Dr. Wendy Mogel (2001) suggests reframing a child's most annoying traits as signs of their biggest strength. Reimagine a picky, nervous, obsessive child as serious and detail-oriented, and a complaining child as discerning. You will be able to reach your students more effectively when you can reframe their negative behaviors and see their weaknesses as masked strengths. Constant complaining could be persistence masked by a whiny voice. What seems like laziness might be evidence of a meditative mind. Messiness could be a sign of a creative spirit. Or, as a colleague of mine discovered, defiance can be forthrightness.

▶ Reframe student defiance

Being able to see a student's negative behavior as a clue to what that student needs can help you reframe defiant behavior and respond to it effectively. Teacher Jennifer Perkins experienced this on her first day of school with her 5th grade class.

After a lesson on the parts of speech, Mrs. Perkins asked the students to introduce themselves with an adjective beginning with the first letter of their first name. For example, she was "Jolly Jennifer." The students' blank stares suggested that many of them didn't know what an adjective was, so she launched into a minilesson before resuming the introductions. The students picked up the idea easily and soon were laughing.

When it was Shante's turn, however, she stood up, looked Mrs. Perkins in the eye, and stated, "I ain't playing no stupid name game." Mrs. Perkins tried encouraging her by making suggestions, such as "Sharp Shante" and "Shy Shante." Shante just rolled her eyes. Not only did she refuse to participate, she refused to sit down when Mrs. Perkins asked her to. "Why don't you come over here and make me?" Shante challenged.

None of Mrs. Perkins's education classes had prepared her for a showdown on the first day of school. But it struck her that what Shante really wanted was to be in control, to assert her power, to have respect. She walked over to the girl and said, "Madame, won't you please sit down?"

"*Madame*, huh?" Shante said. "I like that." She smiled as she spoke, and she sat down. She wasn't embarrassed in front of the other students because she was a *madame;* she felt special.

At the end of the day, the class lined up for dismissal. Suddenly, Shante walked over to Mrs. Perkins, threw her arms around Mrs. Perkins's neck, and said, "That's my hug for the day." For the rest of the year, Mrs. Perkins gave and received hugs from this student— who just needed somebody to notice that she was someone special. Instead of taking Shante's defiance as a personal affront, Mrs. Perkins saw it as a clue to what Shante needed.

▶ Challenge students' low expectations of themselves

Students who have become dispirited either float into the classroom like a balloon low on helium or dart around it like a squirrel caught in a pillowcase. Either way, these students need focused attention from you. If you can relate this attention to the curriculum, then you and the student both win.

Mrs. Sanders, a 7th grade teacher, recognized that many of her female students entered her class with the same struggle: they were nonreaders who identified strongly with the negative descriptions that their peers gave them. Instead of fighting the negative labels ("dummy" or "easy"), these girls accepted it as their truth. Mrs. Sanders knew that simply telling the girls to try harder in school and ignore what their peers said about them wouldn't work, so she chose an unconventional approach. She finds high-interest, modern, easier stories with characters similar to the girls for them to read together as a group. As the students identify with characters from a comfortable distance and see the characters make changes in themselves, they begin to see that they, too, can make changes in their lives. Mrs. Sanders doesn't insist that they talk about their own lives in the discussions in class, but in her essay assignments, she offers various avenues to help students connect with the characters and create long-term plans for themselves based on what they learned from the characters.

I've used similar assignments to highlight a quality that I would like to see my students work toward, such as perseverance. Figure 4.1 shows one such assignment, in which I aimed to inspire my

Figure 4.1

Sample Assignment: Communicating the Power of Perseverance

The Easy Way? NEVER! Winners Who Refused to Quit

Directions:
1. Read the words of the following successful people.
2. Pick one person and research that person's failures and successes.
3. Complete the exercises below, describing your chosen person.

Lance Armstrong: "Pain is temporary. It may last a minute, or an hour, or a day, or a year, but eventually it will subside and something else will take its place. If I quit, however, it lasts forever."

Winston Churchill: "Never give in, never give in, never, never, never, never, never—in nothing, great or small, large or petty—never give in except to convictions of honor and good sense. Never, never, never, never give up."

Walt Disney: "If you can dream it, you can do it."

Carl Lewis: "Remembering that you have both wins and losses along the way, I don't take either one too seriously."

Charles Darwin: "I was considered by all my masters and my father a very ordinary boy, rather below the common standard of intellect."

Albert Einstein: "Intellectual growth should commence at birth and cease only at death."

Helen Keller: "When one door of happiness closes, another opens; but often we look so long at the closed door that we do not see the one which has been opened for us."

Michael Jordan: "I've failed over and over again in my life. That is why I succeed."

Madame Curie: "Life is not easy for any of us. But what of that? We must have perseverance and above all confidence in ourselves. We must believe that we are gifted for something, and that this thing, at whatever cost, must be attained."

Vince Lombardi: "It's not whether you get knocked down; it's whether you get back up."

Ralph Baer: The inventor of home video games claims to be too busy thinking to talk about how he was so successful.

Famous person:

Home life:

Special abilities:

Race or ethnicity:
Religion:
Socioeconomic status:

Goals and dreams:

Failures:

Successes:

This person is like me because . . .

I can be successful just like this person because . . .

_____

students by introducing them to famous people who experienced profound failure before they met with success.

Connecting Parents' Background to Curricula

Most people love to talk about what they've experienced in their life, even if those experiences are negative. Getting to know the families in your classroom allows you to create more effective invitations to engagement—ones that acknowledge and respect the people they are and the values they hold. The strategies that I propose give you opportunities to communicate invitations in covert ways that welcome parents and help them feel comfortable in a school setting.

▶ Do your research

Start by gathering basic demographic information about the parents who refuse your invitations to involvement. Then go deeper. What are their occupations? Where is the family from? What do they do for fun? What are they most proud of? Solicit this information in one-on-one discussions with parents. You can also send home a survey with the title "Tell Me About Your Family." Seek information that will help color in the details of your students' home lives, and then use this information as hooks to use in future invitations for parents to become engaged. For example, a survey response from a parent who has never volunteered before might show that the parent is a geologist. Right then and there, tack a note in your science book to invite this parent to come talk about rocks with your 4th grade students when you get to that unit.

▶ Use bulletin boards to spotlight families

What you put on your bulletin board shows students what is important to you. When parents come into the classroom, they soak in the details on your walls and bulletin boards. Plant seeds of welcome that will silently summon them to accept your invitations to become engaged in their child's academic life. I've had great success "showcasing" students' families on my bulletin board, a move that communicates to students that I value them and their families. When parents pass by the bulletin board and see one family's handiwork, they feel a connection between school and family. This connection shows that your invitations are sincere and that you truly believe that families have worthwhile ideas to contribute to the school environment. This might be just what parents need to see before they will say yes to becoming involved.

Whether a teacher's inquiry into a family's background resonates for the family for one day or leads to many instances of parent involvement, gaining an understanding of each student's family will help connect the dots of the school-parent-child triangle.

How to Handle Conflict Without Undoing All the Work You've Done to Establish Connections

The first time I had to say "no" to a student, my heart pounded and my fingers clenched. I was nervous that I wasn't making the right choice and that the student would refuse any further engagement in my class. This is a pretty standard response to confrontation. I still feel a little uncomfortable whenever I have to direct a student's behavioral choices or discuss an issue with a parent, but now, I anticipate this reaction and see it as proof that I still care about my students. If I didn't care, I certainly wouldn't feel anxiety about assigning students to a "working lunch" or creating a plan of action for parents of failing students. Instead of avoiding confrontation or simply glossing over a problem, I have created set consequences and routines for situations that I come across regularly.

Setting Consequences (and Showing Students How to Think Them Through)

Devising consequences to rule breaking and off-task behavior is a job that should be undertaken with a high level of seriousness because of the permanency of students' records, especially as they enter high school.

▶ Be clear about rules and expectations

I have two rules of thumb on this subject. The first is to create classroom rules, expectations, and consequences that I really believe in. The second is to always respect my students.

Imagine your ideal classroom. Is it quiet or noisy? Messy or neat? Are the desks in straight rows or clusters? Then consider your students and how they fit into your scene. The more comfortable and confident you are in the classroom structure you create, the more likely your students are to adapt to your environment.

Take the time to communicate your rules, expectations, and consequences. Explain to students how their choices will directly affect their grades. You will always have students who believe they are above the rules and have to be made into believers. If you create consequences that you can defend and stay true to, you will motivate students to meet your curricular expectations and help them understand that they, too, must follow the rules.

▶ Be as good as your word

You will always have students who will need convincing that you will carry out consequences as promised. Some students float through school with Jedi-like powers that exude the sentiment "I am above the rules." Don't fall under their spell, for once students see you let one consequence slide, they will feel as if every one of your consequences will slide.

My consequences were challenged one winter quarter by two of our school's star basketball players. These students were used to being treated with privilege on campus, and they were surprised to learn they had each earned an *F* for the quarter. They were now ineligible for sports, and in their minds, I had personally kicked them off the basketball team. Each asked for extra credit and for me to round up their grade. I responded by encouraging them to try harder the next quarter. Both left my classroom very upset, but I was confident that I had done the right thing.

That afternoon, the students returned with Coach Turner by their side. As we sat down to chat, I felt a bit like a teacher in a Lifetime movie, about to be pressured to inflate star athletes' grades.

"Coach Turner," I said, "I imagine you are concerned about the choice these two students have made."

"You mean their choice to fail?"

"Yes."

He looked over to the boys. "So what happened?"

Tony said, "She doesn't like us. This is just a regular class, and she works us too hard."

Coach said, "Oh, I get it. She has high expectations—higher than the expectations you have for yourselves. Is that right, Ms.

Ridnouer?" Then he asked with a wink, "Or do you just have it out for these boys?"

"Coach, I expect an awful lot of these boys because I know they have a lot to give."

Coach replied, "Sounds reasonable enough to me."

The students looked dejected. Their plan of Coach bullying me into raising their grade hadn't worked. The four of us hammered out a plan for Tony and Dominique to come to me for their average on a regular basis, so they could be sure they'd raise their grades and regain their eligibility. For the rest of the school year, they did as well in my class as they did on the court. Sticking to my grading plan and communicating it in a calm and compassionate way in partnership with Coach Turner brought about a resolution that in turn brought about personal and academic growth for the students.

"Conferencing a Solution" with Parents

All teachers have experienced that watershed moment where a minor problem in student behavior, effort, or achievement is at risk of turning into a major problem. This is the time to act. Instead of letting punishments add up or allowing the behavior or habit to become more ingrained, ask for a conference with the student and the student's parents to communicate your interest in resolving the issue immediately. Waiting to communicate with parents until after you have been dealing with a bad behavior for two months could lead to impatience and frustration steering the conference, instead of compassion and clear vision.

▶ Open with the positive

Begin with a description of the student's positive attributes to communicate to the parents that you care about the student and truly want to help him or her make better choices. This will help the parents relax and focus on the problem instead of their reaction to the teacher.

▶ Keep the focus on the problem

I maintain a log that I use to track negative behavioral patterns in students that I am concerned about. The log serves as documentation that paves the way for special services if I suspect that a student might need them. It also serves as evidence that I care for my students enough to take the time to monitor a potential problem.

As you reach the point in the conference where you present the concern that you have for the student, be prepared for excuses from the student, the parents, or both. It's easy to get offended or to readily accept excuses when they are given. More effective than either of those responses is to choose to recognize these responses as coping strategies, not solutions. Respond in a way that deals directly with the problem. For example, a student who is talking out of turn in class might defend herself by saying, "Jane always talks to me first. It would be rude not to answer her." Instead of discussing whether Jane truly starts the conversation or whether it is rude to ignore chatty Jane, focus on the problem by saying, "We are not here to place blame on anyone. We are here to discuss how we can focus your attention on your classwork."

A parent hearing criticism of her child might complain, "I can't stand it when someone thinks after working with my child for one month that she knows how to help him more than I do." You must remain calm when these kinds of accusations are thrown around. Focusing on the goal—improving the student's behavior, so he can achieve academically—will help you respond in a way that encourages partnership instead of argument. A response such as, "I can appreciate where you are coming from. I wouldn't like it either if I thought a teacher thought she knew my child better than I did. How would you respond to this behavior at home?" Listening to students and parents alike will not only help build trust among conference participants but also help resolve concerns. These conferences can also serve as a positive source of attention for the student that might, over time, cause the need for negative attention-seeking behaviors to dissipate.

Making the Case for Sharing Concerns and Skills

Students and parents alike have concerns that stop them from being engaged, but they don't always speak up. Most teachers have noted how students' firmly held ideas of what they can and cannot do leaves them reluctant to take risks or step outside the limits they've set for themselves. It's the same with parents, who might label themselves as "uneducated," "disabled," "the single mom," "the young parent," "the poor parent," "the stutterer," or "the dummy." They might believe that this is how everyone else sees them, too—a distorted perception that can lead them to remove themselves from the group of parents that they see as "the engaged ones."

Although such parents are unlikely to discuss these beliefs with you, they tend to communicate them in other ways—the same kinds of comments and body language that can clue you in to students' academic or personal issues and beliefs. With both groups, the key is to be open to discussing these concerns and have some suggestions at the ready to address them effectively.

Turning a Negative Experience into a Positive One

The first step in a new direction is almost always the toughest one to take, meaning that if you can get students to think differently about a behavior or a challenge, the hardest part of the job has been handled. When you notice a problem—perhaps students talking or trying to text during a lesson—stop what you're doing and discuss how small, everyday choices can have a big impact on learning. When students get frustrated, encourage them to focus on the "how" of a task instead of the "if" of a task. When they view mistakes and occasional frustration as necessary steps in learning, students become more willing to work through those steps. "Microteaching" of this sort highlights the importance of the lesson, garnering both student attention and respect.

▶ Teach students to look for specific obstacles and develop a plan

Even the most motivated students get "stuck" sometimes. If you can figure out what is preventing one student's progress and find a solution, you just might be able to find a tool that will benefit many students in the class.

I once taught a student named Brian who sailed through all work until the day we worked on parallel sentence structure. It turned out that everything we had covered up to that point were concepts Brain had been taught before, and he didn't know how to digest this new material. Now, Brian didn't tell me this in words, but he didn't need to. His body language was hard to miss. He had gone from sitting up with his eyes focused on me to slumping down in his seat with his hood on. I stopped the lesson and asked Brian how he was doing with the material.

"Man, I just don't get it," he admitted. "I am frustrated!"

I thought for a moment. This was a teachable moment if there ever was one. "You know what?" I said, "This is a great opportunity, Brian. Now you know what frustration looks like and feels like. You can recognize it when it arrives. So now, all you have to do is come up with a plan for handling it."

I went on to tell the class that, as a runner, I experience frustration every time I lace up my running shoes. I expect to hate running until about the fourth mile. Until that fourth mile, I am wondering, "What the heck am I doing out here? Running stinks." My body is wondering, too. My chest hurts; my knees hurt. It's too cold; it's too hot. But I don't let the frustration stop me, because I have a plan: to make it to Mile Four. I promise myself that if after I've run four miles I still feel this way, then I will stop. And the fact is that by the time I reach Mile Four, the struggle has always gone away. I feel as though I could run forever.

What I wanted to do with Brian is point out that frustration is something he could accept as part of the learning process, not the unsuccessful end of learning or something to be ashamed of. Once he knew to look for frustration as something to expect, he would be ready with a plan. In his case, he decided the plan would be to ask me to explain the idea a different way. The entire class witnessed not only Brian's "aha!" moment but also the way he put tools in place to accomplish what he needed to. They also started asking me to phrase an idea a new way or asking classmates to help them understand a concept. Frustration became a starting point instead of an end point.

▶ Help students recognize and respond to their frustration

I want to offer a particular strategy related to frustration because I've found it is the most common enemy of student engagement. Frustration is really what's going on when you hear a student complain, "I just don't get it!" or when a student turns on you and says, "You don't get me!" It's often what's leading students to sit silently and seethe with anger or melt into sadness. A 2nd grader crying during math time, a 7th grader crossing his arms angrily, and a 10th grader refusing to participate in group discussions are each showing frustration.

You can meet these responses with an action plan based on giving them tools to break through this barrier to learning and reengage with the content.

Ideas for Students Who Respond to Frustration with Anger

• Give them a chance to save face and calm down by allowing them to sit at a desk in the hallway until they feel ready to rejoin the class.

• Ask them who they would like to partner with when they become frustrated, and encourage them to work with a partner when they need to.

• Teach them how to cope with negative feelings by giving them permission to pace in the back of the room (out of the line of sight of other students) to work off some of the angry energy.

Ideas for Students Who Respond to Frustration with Sadness

• Help them give voice to their sadness by asking them to create a dialogue between two imaginary characters who are trying to learn the day's lesson.

• Incorporate kinesthetic activities into your lessons as a way to get withdrawn students up, moving, and engaged in positive action.

• Allow them to be responsible for something, whether it be watering the class plant, wiping down the desks, or keeping the pencils sharpened. This shows them that sustained attention and care will bring about positive results.

▶ Help students shake their past and focus on the present

Students' past experiences can blind them to opportunities to learn in your classroom. Help them let go of the past, so they can see their present as the gift that it is. I do this by encouraging them to share their feelings about the subject in a letter to me. Once I've read the letters, I respond to each student's concerns personally. The key to this technique is not to deny students' struggles but rather to assure them that you are there to help them.

I had a student, Casey, who wrote to me that he was not sure he would do well in my class because he did not like to read or write. He worried that because he lacked spelling and grammatical skills, people would judge him and make him "feel like a fool." In response, I created a support system that focused on improving his weaknesses and highlighting his strengths. Casey dove right into his assignments and took advantage of the learning center that our school offered. I assigned essay topics that asked him about his personal history, and he worked on the assignments until he had articulated his story accurately, producing a humorous essay about his experiences playing war games and a somber essay about his experience with the Boy Scouts. The struggles he had experienced with spelling and grammar fell away as he concentrated on the content first and the mechanics second. He had been so wrapped up in worrying about the mechanics of writing that he had thought himself as incapable of the expressive elements of writing. He easily earned an *A* in the class, and his faith in his identity as a writer was restored. Casey needed to be able to see his abilities unclouded by fear and doubt. Once the clouds were blown away through practice and hard work, he was able to recognize his writing as quality work.

Tapping the Power of Parents' Concerns and Skills

The more parents use the word "volunteer" to describe themselves, the more they are willing to commit to actions that reflect this description. Research by Holland, Lachicotte, Skinner, and Cain (2001) stresses the importance of identity: "People tell others who they are, but even more important, they tell themselves and then try to act as though they are who they say they are. These under-standings, especially those with strong emotional resonance for the teller, are what we refer to as identities. Identities are the key means by which people care about and care for what is going on around them" (p. 3)

Find out how your parents identify themselves and you will find a key to encouraging them to accept your invitations. Partner their identities with an awareness of common excuses for not being engaged, and you will be able to preplan some strategic solutions.

In a study supported by the Bill and Melinda Gates Foundation (Bridgeland, Dilulio, Streeter, & Mason, 2008), researchers found that most parents who identify themselves as "less involved than they should be" identified time conflicts as the primary reason. Other reasons these parents cited included lack of information, lack of communication, lack of knowledge of what is going on, and a need for more contact from the school.

▶ Use the excuses parents provide to inform your next round of invitations

Parents' demurrals or explanations for why they don't think they can become involved in your classroom offer valuable insight and can guide you to the kind of involvement that would be doable for them. Here are a few excuses I've heard again and again, along with some suggested replies:

"I'm Too Busy"

• Offer an opportunity to support the classroom at home by collating classroom materials.

• Ask if their employer gives time off for volunteer work.

• Suggest alternative times for becoming involved. This could include before school, at lunchtime, or after school.

"I'm Not a Teacher"

• Invite parents into the classroom to observe you in a reading lesson and then ask them to read with a small group of students on their own.

• Organize a charity car wash or other nonacademic event to attract those parents who might not feel qualified to teach a lesson or become a member of the school leadership team.

"I Have Nothing to Contribute"

• Ask what parents are comfortable doing and find volunteer opportunities that utilize those skill sets. For example, a parent who enjoys computers could be asked to work with a small group of students learning how to use new software. Similarly, a parent who likes to knit can be encouraged to lead a knitting workshop after school.

"I'm New to the School and Don't Know What I'm Doing"

• Make parents aware of workshops, seminars, and meetings that will acclimate them to the school and build their comfort in contributing to the school.

• Offer to partner parents with "seasoned" engaged parents on an upcoming task that you know will utilize their skill sets.

"I Never Know What's Going On"

- Provide the school's web address and directions on how to receive the school newsletter along with your own contact details, so this parent can receive class and school information directly.

- Send reminders home with all students, so parents know exactly what is needed by you and the school at large.

▶ Keep your door open to parents

When my middle son, James, came home from kindergarten one day talking about Native Americans, I listened happily. He knew all sorts of facts and was very animated in his recounting of what he had learned. I encouraged his storytelling and was pleased that he found their culture so interesting. I sat down that night and wrote his teacher a note explaining a bit about my experience working on the Cheyenne River Reservation in South Dakota and volunteered to come in some day to talk to the class, read a story, and bring in some authentic fry bread for the children to try. She was thrilled and asked me to come in a day later.

Another kindergarten class joined my James's class, so I had 40 5- and 6-year-olds at my feet in the story circle. They asked a lot of questions and enjoyed the story. I was thrilled to share my story and felt even more comfortable with my son's teacher. This activity was a meaningful way for me to contribute to the classroom, and I felt welcome. My son received the message that I think school and learning are important, and showing him this message was a thousand times more effective than merely telling him.

Parents' stories give weight to the words they speak to their children. Invite parents into your classroom to share their stories when they relate to curricular items. The parents can serve to reinforce your lessons because of the respect with which children hold the words of adults who take the time to speak with them.

There Is Opportunity Within a Struggle

People are born learners. They are eager to tackle problems and even more eager to create solutions, as long as they have somebody to listen to them and encourage them. Keep in mind, though, that they don't always come out and tell you how they are feeling. Recently, I was working with a student on a creative writing assignment. She hadn't completed the assignment and was listing the many reasons why she wouldn't be able to finish it. I watched her shaky hands smooth back her curly hair, and listened to her produce excuse after excuse. When she stopped to take a breath, I said, "It sounds as if you are feeling overwhelmed and need to complete this assignment in steps." Relief washed over her face. Articulating her feelings made the feelings OK for her to have. She was then able to develop a plan for approaching each section separately and was eager to get back to work.

Try putting a name to the feelings that are stopping your students and their parents from being engaged, and then help them create a plan to manage that emotion. Freeing them of the negative emotion will oftentimes enable them to see that they are indeed capable of being engaged.

Interpersonal Responses

Each school year is a journey during which effective teachers develop relationships with the students and parents who make up their classroom community. As teachers come to understand who the students and parents are as people, they create and share tools that support participation and cultivate an environment that optimizes engagement. They work with students and parents "where they are" rather than "where they should be," and accept both the joys and the complications this philosophy brings.

Effective teachers work to orchestrate all the notes emerging from their diverse students and parents into a vibrant, harmonious whole. This acceptance and appreciation of the classroom community helps to build student and parent buy-in and boost their willingness to accept teacher invitations to learning and involvement. In Chapters 5 and 6, we look at the essential aspects of cultivating interpersonal responses to students and parents: creating relationships and fostering participation.

Creating Relationships

We don't accomplish anything in this world alone...
and whatever happens is the result of the whole tapestry
of one's life and all the weavings of individual threads
from one to another that creates something.

✳ SANDRA DAY O'CONNOR ✳

Successful teachers create relationships with students and parents by sharing themselves: their time, their expertise, and sometimes, their monetary and interpersonal resources. By inviting students and parents into your life in this way, you are recognizing their need for personal communication and interaction. And the more they can relate to you—as both a professional leader and a person—the easier it is for them to trust you, relax their fears about failure, and engage in the school.

In this chapter, we will focus on how to create engagement-promoting relationships with students and parents. Here are the key questions:

1. How does sharing your experiences help you partner with students and their parents?

2. What are some motivational tools you can pass on to students and parents?

3. What are some motivational ways to promote understanding?

How Sharing Your Experience Promotes Partnership

Every day we stand in front of our students recounting the importance of getting a head start on a project and staying on top of assignments, but oftentimes, our words go unheeded. Many students have to touch the flame to know they will get burned. They have to see for themselves that they don't produce their best work when it's thrown together the night before instead of consistently attended to over a few weeks. But even as you warn your students of the dangers of procrastination and give them examples of students who have failed your class in the past, you know that the next day you will be standing ready with salve to soothe the pain of those students who did not heed your advice.

Don't rest there. Strive to proactively create opportunities for your students to stretch themselves and take risks within the safe, supportive confines of your classroom to build their logical reasoning, self-awareness, and confidence (skills all people need to function well). One way to do this is by sharing your own successes and failures with your students to communicate that all humans struggle, that this is something you understand, and that you are there to address their struggle and create strategies to work through it. They still may not follow your advice, but they just might adapt your advice to suit their personalities and learning styles to create a way to complete assignments and attack challenges that magnifies their strengths and minimizes their weaknesses.

Perhaps you've wondered how much of yourself you should share with your students and their parents as you attempt to engage them in and out of the classroom. I have found that the more honest I am and the more often I share stories about my own challenges and successes, the more willing my students and their parents are to accept my invitations of engagement. This has especially been the case when they come from cultural backgrounds that are different from my own. My stories serve to build cultural bridges that lead to acceptance of engagement opportunities.

Showing Yourself as a "Real Person"

Students want to know the person behind the identity of "teacher." Don't be afraid to share different versions of yourself. Let them know about your interests, the different job titles that you have held, and tidbits from your childhood that they can relate to.

▶ Share your academic stories

A teacher's "academic" self can be an inspiration and motivation to students. When I told my high school students about the college professor who said that my paper was so bad that I didn't even deserve an *F,* my students didn't care that I was an adult or that we came from different cultural backgrounds; they simply felt bad for me and were curious to find out how I responded to the professor. This gave me the chance to find out about my students; I turned the question back to them, asking, "Well, what would you have done?" They told me that they would have walked out or would have "demanded a do-over." Some said they wouldn't have known what to do. All of these responses were helpful, giving me insight into how these students might respond to failure or embarrassment in my class.

From there, we proceeded to a larger discussion about handling conflict. I started by telling them that initially, I accepted this professor's assessment of my writing, figuring that I just wasn't any good. Then, after another essay was returned with a poor mark, I got mad. I ripped it up and asked the professor if I could resubmit both papers. I wrote and rewrote until I felt confident in my work, earning an *A* on those papers and on every paper in that class after that. I chose not to accept this professor's assessment and to work to earn a revised assessment.

This conversation humanized me to my students and showed them that I was interested in being a responsive teacher, mindful of their perspectives and interested in the people they were and the ways they thought about things.

▶ Be the accessible expert

Present yourself as an authority who is available and willing to help your students find their way. As a certified teacher, you have what the students don't have—credentials. Share these with your students to give them pegs to hang their questions on. A colleague of mine, Ms. Thompson, teaches a high school course for students considering the medical profession as a career. On the first day of school each year, she introduces herself to her students as a registered nurse with a bachelor's degree in nursing, establishing herself as a professional source of information about nursing. She then inquires about the careers students would like to pursue in the future, bringing immediacy to the fact that her class is a bridge to their future. Her disclosure develops a connection with students, and they trust that she will guide them toward a career that matches their skill set and their interests.

▶ Talk about finding strength in a perceived weakness

Sometimes it is your life experience that gives you the credentials the students need to confidently approach your lesson. Ms. Nelson, a geometry teacher in a high-poverty high school, recognizes herself in the faces and actions of many of her minority students. She is an active member of the African-American community and works to build on the community's strengths while counteracting its weaknesses. One such weakness is domestic violence. Ms. Nelson has survived an abusive marriage, and she wants her students to also be survivors. She shares her experience with her students to illustrate to them how her choices affected her life. She talks about how she had to learn how to value herself, because she wants her students to value themselves enough that they won't tolerate mistreatment from themselves or from others.

Sharing this information with students might raise the ire of a few parents who wish to shelter their kids from the truth of scary adulthood. But Ms. Nelson is prepared for parents who ask how her situation relates to math class. She explains, "Math involves figuring out problems in a logical fashion, and so does trying to get out of an abusive marriage. The more we can teach our students how to use their minds in a calm, rational fashion, the better they will do in all their classes, during testing situations, and in personal relationships."

Because of their shared understanding of Ms. Nelson's past, her students bond tightly, and this cohesion builds a rapport that is beneficial in group discussions and projects. However, this cohesion is an auxiliary benefit, and not her primary goal. She would like her life lessons to circle back to the students, and she hopes that their relationship with a survivor who is thriving will help them recognize the conditions they need to thrive as well.

Being a Respectful Peer to Parents

Like most people who are not educators themselves, your students' parents are likely to have mixed feelings about teachers, some positive and some negative. I have taught many students whose parents had unhappy experiences in school and saw teachers as judges— people who saw them as "less than." I learned to create opportunities for us to interact in ways that would help them to see me as an individual and would allow me to demonstrate the value I placed on their insights and contributions. As potentially powerful contributors to their child's academic achievement, all parents need the chance to understand and gain command of tools they might use to partner with teachers and drive home learning.

▶ Problem solve together

Consider inviting groups of parents in for an action-focused meeting to look at curricular issues or to address specific, of-the-moment issues, such as cell phone policy, dress code, or gum chewing. Here are some sample topics for parent meetings, complete with some model descriptions.

Elementary School Level

• *Hints for Handwriting*: We will discuss how to judge your child's handwriting, when poor handwriting might suggest a concern, and what you can do to improve your child's handwriting.

• *Supporting Good Reading Habits*: We will discuss daily habits that lead to lifelong reading.

• *Everyday Math Practice*: Whether you are in the grocery store or the soccer field, there is always a mathematical challenge to be found. In this meeting, we will look at how to create math problems to share with your child at home.

Middle School Level

• *Encouraging Argument (at Least on Paper!)*: This meeting is designed to give you simple steps for helping your child craft effective persuasive essays.

• *Middle School Math 101*: This meeting is for all parents who are feeling less than confident when your child comes to you for help and could use a refresher course in middle school math topics.

• *Organization Station*: We will discuss the basic expectations for all middle school students and some practical tips in how you can help your child develop habits so that he or she is able to successfully meet these expectations.

High School Level

• *Study Skills*: This meeting is an overview of how long homework should take each night, the supplies the students need, and the space that encourages effective studying and homework completion.

• *Addressing Math Wrath:* We will discuss strategies for encouraging your child when he or she becomes frustrated with math. This will include information on where to find help online and through my class website, what to do if the student is overwhelmed, and what to say when your child feels like giving up.

• *Reading, Writing, and Thinking (Oh My!):* In this meeting, I will provide an overview of the reading and writing plan for the year, my expectations for student work, and what you can do to support your child's learning throughout the school year.

Meetings like these send the message that you honor the parents' role as partners in their child's education. They also communicate to parents that they are not alone in the difficulties they might be facing with their children, which is a message that can build community and increase parents' willingness to volunteer.

▶ **Set up workshops for parents and students to attend together**

When you hear clamoring from students about particular topics, issues, or worries, think about planning a workshop that students might attend with their parents to address that topic. Yes, sometimes students' airing of concerns is just banter to pass the time rather than something that warrants a swift and informed response, but I believe taking these concerns seriously is a way to demonstrate respect. I invite students and their parents to come in for an open forum where we can all work together to learn about and resolve particular issues. Here are some sample workshop topics for students and their parents:

Elementary School Level
- How to Stop a Bully
- Television Viewing and Its Effect on Learning
- All About Our School's Reading Program
- How to Help Your Child with Math
- How to Help your Child with Writing
- Effective Discipline

- Effective Communication in the Family
- Exercise for Everyone

Middle and High School Levels
- Empowering Adolescent Girls
- Sensitizing Adolescent Boys
- How to Help with Homework
- Improving Math Skills
- Improving Reading Skills
- Relationships
- Conflict Resolution
- How to Talk to a Teenager
- How to Find Out What Is Happening at the High School
- School Success After a Suspension
- Everyday Etiquette

In addition to giving students and their parents the resources they need to address concerns, these workshops help parents and teachers form a relationship, and they familiarize parents with the classroom environment. When you create a series of workshops in response to concerns shared by parents, you are waving a banner that says, "Parent engagement isn't a one-shot affair. Parent engagement is an ongoing, much-valued process."

Workshops don't require a lot of money (especially if they make use of resources your school already has, including computers and athletic equipment), but they require intangible assets: time, motivation, and vision. In my experience, though, the energy expended in furthering teacher-parent partnerships is energy well spent. Consider, too, that workshops offer a perfect opportunity to expand your volunteer ranks. At the close of a workshop, I recommend taking a few minutes to bring up explicit concerns you have and ask parents for their assistance. For example, an elementary school teacher might explain that students have been struggling with learning new vocabulary words and solicit a few parent volunteers to create sets of practice flash cards. The teacher could also ask parents to dedicate time for reviewing vocabulary words with their children and encourage parents not in attendance to do the same. The common goal will promote the feeling of community and support curricular aims.

Motivational Tools to Pass on to Students and Parents

Children rely on the adults around them to provide models for how they should approach academic challenges. Stanford University psychologist Carol Dweck has studied the words and actions that parents use in search of those tools that are the most effective. In her research (Blackwell, Trzesniewski, & Dweck, 2007), Dweck discovered that an emphasis on effort is an effective means of motivating students, and she concluded that children who are praised for being smart tend to give up easily because they don't have the coping skills to manage the effort that more difficult problems require. Children who are praised for effort, however, are more likely to be energized and willing to tackle tougher problems. These words and actions are most effective when they correlate with ones students have heard and seen in the past. A catchy phrase, such as "Your 'I Can' is more important than your 'IQ,'" is similar to "Never give up"—something they might have heard from another teacher or their parents.

You can also offer parents effective tools for motivating their children to achieve. Sometimes what parents most need to know is how to address an academic concern when it arises. The goal is to steer parents away from negative responses ("You'll never get into college with grades like that!") and toward words that will help their children see that success is achievable.

Using Mottoes to Inspire Student Achievement

In my classroom, mottoes are like church bells in a small town—they are repeated often enough to provide clear direction. My students hear me say, "Carpe Diem" and "There is no 'I' in team" throughout the year, and they invariably come to incorporate these mottoes into their own work. Although students tease me about my repeated *bon mots,* after a while they accept the nudge of "Hustle your bustle," and English language learners follow my lead by adding "yet" to the end of the sentence "I can't speak English." Mottoes are effective because they are short and easy to remember, and they provide a frame for students' perspectives. Here are some ways you might incorporate mottoes into your instruction.

▶ Use mottoes to break barriers

Students who are struggling sometimes use negative behavior as a form of protection. Incorporating mottoes that express your ideals creates opportunity for students to forget their need for protection, if only momentarily. A moment is all you need to move into a student's world and help him or her see it in a new, more productive way. One day Sheena responded to my "Good morning!" with "Who are you to tell me what kind of morning it is?" When I heard those words, I knew she needed some tools to help her thrive. I started responding to Sheena's negative words with "You're so much better than that." I saw a flicker of light when I said this, and I knew I had found a way in.

Shortly after this, I met with Sheena's mother. I showed her evidence of inspired writing in Sheena's work, and then I shared my concern about how Sheena's negative outlook could color her whole day. My goal was to learn more about Sheena and her family and to share some tools. I talked about how I had started responding to Sheena with "You're so much better than that," and Sheena's mother smiled. I asked her if she would be able to incorporate this motto into her own dialogue with Sheena. She agreed and seemed relieved that I wasn't there to tell her how bad her child was. Over the course of the school year, Sheena began to change. She still came to school in a bad mood every once in a while, but when something negative came out of her mouth, she knew she would hear, "You're so much better than that" in response. She began to accept that she had control over her attitude, she became so much more than the nasty person she had been allowing herself to be, and she became an *A* student to boot.

▶ Create your own list of mottoes

Ask any successful person what motivates them and you'll often hear, "Well, my father always said…" or "Grandma always told me.…" Ask yourself what motivates you, and take a few minutes to generate your own mottoes to use in the classroom with students and to share with parents. In addition, consider incorporating a few of the following mottoes into your everyday interactions with students:

- Don't look back.
- *Crescit eundo.* (It grows as it goes.)
- Who dares, wins.
- *Per ardua ad astra.* (Through adversity to the stars.)
- *Citius, altius, fortius.* (Swifter, higher, stronger [the motto of the Olympics].)
- When you're through changing, you're through.
- Make the most of yourself, for that is all there is of you.
- This too shall pass.
- Great minds discuss ideas, average minds discuss events, and small minds discuss people.
- Anger is only one letter short of danger.
- If it is to be, it is up to me.

Getting Parents into the Motivational Game

A fresh perspective just might be what parents need to catch their breath in nurturing their child. Perhaps the parents are stuck in their relationship with their child, feeling that no matter what they say or do, their child will still argue at homework time, whine about cleaning, and moan about bedtime. Give parents some tools to use before there is a problem with their child and their adrenaline is running too high to absorb your advice.

▶ Share mottoes directly with parents

Knowing what to say and when to say it is priceless information for parents who feel the divide between youth and adulthood every day. Give parents the advantage of your exposure to young people by sharing the currency of your classroom—the mottoes you use to motivate your students. Post them on your class or grade-level website, include them in your class newsletter, write them in the margins of homework assignments, and use them in conversation with individual parents. Many of the mottoes might be similar to words that parents use at home, but when students hear the same motto at home and at school, they just might begin to digest its meaning.

If you like, you might extend the impact of your mottoes (and those created by parents and students) by encouraging other teachers and staff members to adopt them in their communication with students and parents. The mottoes can be put in the school newsletter, incorporated into homework assignments, and displayed on posters throughout the school. You might even ask local civic groups, churches, and banks with changeable signs to post these mantras so students will encounter these motivational thoughts and encouragement wherever they go in the community.

Motivational Ways to Promote Understanding

As the poet Mark Van Doren put it, "Nothing in man is more serious than his sense of humor; it is the sign that he wants all the truth." Teachers who take the time to incorporate humor in their classroom communications relay to students and parents that they truly want students to learn and their subject matter is worth learning. Both students and parents need to feel understood before they will willingly collaborate on a learning challenge or discuss academic concerns. I have found that showing students that I possess a sense of humor makes them more willing to connect what they already know with what I am trying to teach. It shows them that although there are differences between us, there are also similarities. If students can laugh at the same jokes as their teacher, they can also solve the same problems and understand the same literature.

Engaging Students and Parents Through Humor

Using humor in the classroom is a method that motivates students to learn, enhances group cohesion, and diffuses potentially tense situations if used in a positive manner. When a teacher focuses on the good qualities in her students and responds to subject matter in a light, playful way, students feel invited into the lesson in a warm, safe manner. As Barbara Fredrickson (2001) found, "positive emotions (a) broaden people's thought-action repertoires, (b) undo lingering negative emotions, (c) fuel psychological resilience, and (d) build psychological resilience and trigger upward spirals toward enhanced emotional well-being" (p. 224). The takeaway here is that when students face challenging situations, the positive emotions of humor tend to open students up where they might otherwise shut down, helping them to shake off doubt in their abilities, giving them strength to continue when they flounder, and pushing them to feel good about themselves. Your cheerful words paired with open, inviting body language communicate your desire to connect with your students and to connect the curricular content with them as well.

Tomlinson (1999) suggests that a combination of humor and creativity helps students make unexpected and pleasurable connections. Humor can't be taught, but it can be appreciated. Listen to what makes your students laugh or perks up their interest, and find a way to connect it to your lesson in a creatively funny way. The students might say you're corny, or they might think you're cool. Either way, they'll see the connection you are trying to make and come to understand that topic a little bit better. Take advantage of the quick pace of your students' minds and actions to create lessons that sneak in learning under the guise of fun.

▶ Use humor to build classroom culture

Think about the people you tell jokes to, and you will probably draw up a list of friends and family members who are part of your social network. Build this kind of social network in your classroom by incorporating humor regularly in your classroom. Encourage students to connect with their classmates through humor, and you will build a culture that can only be found within your four walls—one that the students will be happy to join.

A talented comedian makes his stand-up routine look spontaneous, but that doesn't mean the routine isn't well rehearsed. The same is true with humor in the classroom. Be prepared with content-related jokes, overheads, and videos that you can cue up on a moment's notice, such as when students' interest begins to wane or when you need humor to bring about that "I got it!" moment. The better you get at this, the more you will encourage students to connect humor with what they are learning, foster like-minded thinking, and make learning even more attractive.

Humor educator Joel Goodman (1995) says, "humor and creativity are intimately related—there is a connection between HAHA and AHA" (p. 41). The open, relaxed environments that accompany humor and lightheartedness are conducive to creative demonstrations of topic understanding. Think of how an interpretive dance of metamorphosis in science class or a rap version about solving a quadratic equation in algebra would help both the presenter and the audience consider the subject matter from a different perspective. Think of what it might tell you about students' understanding. Humor can be just the hook you need to create and sustain interest in a lesson.

Ideas for Integrating More Humor into Your Lessons

• Rewrite popular songs to incorporate facts students are learning, or ask students to create the songs themselves. Replacing simple lyrics with content area material will help reinforce the students' memory of the material and make learning fun. For example, set the rules for integers to the tune of "The Macarena."

• Assign pairs of students the task of humorously rewriting a chapter of their textbook, describing a historical event, or recounting a part of their novel. Give extra points for acting out their rewrite in front of the class.

• Share—anonymously, of course—amusing answers past students have provided (e.g., Q: Name the four seasons. A: Salt, pepper, mustard and vinegar; Q: How do you keep milk from going sour? A: Keep it in the cow.). I've found that students get a kick out of hearing what other students their age wrote, and that these funny responses often open their minds and create interest in discovering the "correct" explanations. If anything, the students just might give their answers an additional moment of reflection so that their answer doesn't become one of your "favorite" student answers.

• Use a lighthearted, on-topic cartoon like the one below to introduce a topic and stimulate discussion. (This one is useful for introducing students to the different style of English used in *Romeo and Juliet*.)

© 2007 by Randy Glasbergen.
www.glasbergen.com

"My teacher isn't qualified to teach spelling!
She spells U 'y-o-u'. She spells BRB 'r-e-t-u-r-n'.
She spells BFN 'g-o-o-d-b-y-e'..."

▶ Use jokes to help nonnative speakers

My nonnative students often seem lonely and disconnected from the classroom community. The language barrier doesn't just block their learning; it also blocks their confidence in building relationships in the classroom. They'd rather be silent than risk appearing incompetent in front of their classmates. Humor is a way to help nonnative speakers practice speaking English and feel as though they are truly part of the school. Trachtenberg (1980) points out a number of reasons why jokes are an effective way to promote English practice, which is so essential to language acquisition: jokes are short and rule-governed, they contain a wide range of speech patterns, they are common to all cultures, they are a good way of embodying a culture, and they serve to relax tension.

Leal (1993) offers some strategies for incorporating jokes in the English language learner classroom, suggesting that teachers tell a joke and ask the students to explain the punch line or try giving students part of the joke and ask the students to write their own punch line. You can also have students translate jokes from their native tongue into English. Finally, jokes can be told as a means of introducing grammar rules.

▶ Use humor to connect with parents

Using humor can be seen by parents as an indicator that you are comfortable with them and that you accept them and their child. In this environment, parents will be far more receptive to discussing and addressing academic and behavioral issues concerning their child. Humor tends to chase the "Are you picking on my child?" question from a parent's mind. And it can open the door to step-by-step solutions to issues at home or at school.

Seeing Concerns from a Parent's Point of View

All parents care about their children and want to know how to help when there is a problem. They just don't always know how to go about it. When a student of mine shows signs of struggle in the classroom, I stop and remind myself of those moments I've had with the student when we were able to laugh together and truly "get" one another. I jot these down so that I remember to share these moments when I'm talking with the student's parents about a concern that I have about their child. I want them to know that I care for their child and that I need their engagement to resolve the issue. My goal is to create common ground for us to walk on together as we address and partner with each other and the student to resolve the issue.

▶ Respond with compassion

Talking to parents about a concern is difficult; talking to a parent about a suspected learning difficulty can be downright agonizing because parents can respond with an array of emotions. They might be angry at themselves and wonder how they could not have known. They might be resentful toward you or past teachers for not drawing attention to the issue earlier. They might be apprehensive about the struggle their child will be facing. Assure parents that all children struggle at school at one time or another, whether they have an identifiable learning disability or not. Share your professional knowledge about learning difficulties and the interventions available to assist students to reassure parents that just because their child might learn differently doesn't mean the child won't be able to learn effectively.

▶ Prepare documentation to support your case for concern

Take some time to cull student work that documents the source of your concern. Is poor handwriting ringing your alarm for dyspraxia? Are poor word-attack skills telling you that he might have a reading difficulty? Or is the student finishing her work early and easily, leading you to think she might be gifted? The more documentation you have, the more positive your encounter with the student's parents will be.

Additionally, write down anecdotal evidence of a learning difficulty from your perspective as the student's classroom teacher. Is his handwriting book always "lost"? Does she repeatedly go to the bathroom during reading time? Is he working ahead in his workbooks or bringing books from home for when he finishes? This anecdotal evidence provides details about the individual student that written work alone cannot convey.

Following the steps below will help make the most of your meetings with parents:

Suggested Steps for Conducting an Effective Parent Meeting

1. *Explain the concern.* Share documentation and anecdotal evidence with parents.

2. *Listen.* Emphasize that the meeting is a dialogue between you and the parents. Ask for their perspective, and give them a turn to speak. They will give you insight into how to work with their child, and you will help allay their fears about having a child with a learning difficulty. The more comfortable they become with the idea of their child's challenge, the more effectively they can implement any strategies you give them.

3. *Offer a plan.* Parents need you to be a professional at this point. They need assurances that their child's challenge is treatable. In most cases, a child will need to undergo testing to determine if he or she indeed has a learning difficulty and what it entails. Giving parents the forms to sign to initiate this testing, along with the contact details of the person who will conduct the testing, gives them confidence that you know what you are talking about. Recommend books and websites that address the child's challenge so that parents can become knowledgeable about the impact this challenge might have on their child, both long- and short-term.

4. *Offer your services as a liaison and advocate.* When testing results come back, parents often need assistance interpreting educational jargon related to both the diagnosis and the school's proposed solutions. Encourage parents to meet with other parents and

professionals who work with students similar to their own child. The Learning Disabilities Association of America (www.ldanatl.org) might have an active group in the area that parents could participate in, or they could join a myriad of online groups to get support from people who have experience with both the educational system and with students coping with learning difficulties. If the child's learning difficulty results in receiving an Individualized Education Plan (IEP), help the parents understand their child's rights to a fair education. Share with them the possible services provided and the parameters of appropriate accommodation. Teachers can create a folder of information just for this purpose. Considering that almost three million individuals in the United States ages 6 through 21 have some form of a learning disability and receive special education in school, you can expect as many as 20 percent of your students to have some kind of learning difference (U.S. Department of Education, 2002). You will serve yourself, your students, and their parents well to partner effectively with them to provide the information and early intervention to help students cope with their learning difference.

Finding Common Ground Brings Everyone Together

Sharing with my students that I attended 10 different schools when I was growing up helps them understand me. In addition, it lets them know that I have experience that helps me understand them. So do you. Dig deep for examples from your own life of when you were triumphant or when you failed in order to humanize yourself to both your students and their parents. They will both see that the waters of engagement are safe, and they'll be more encouraged to jump in and join you.

Fostering Participation

Treat people as if they were what they ought to be and you help them to become what they are capable of being.

✳ JOHANN GOETHE ✳

A successful teacher believes that, given a fair chance, each student will succeed and each parent can find a place at the school level to become involved. This "fairness" doesn't mean giving everyone the same opportunities but, rather, giving each student and each parent what they need to succeed. It might mean having a disruptive child sit next to you during a round robin discussion or providing a gifted child with enrichment resources. One parent might need no invitation before offering to volunteer time in the classroom, while another might need multiple contacts to be coaxed to come in for a conference.

The strategies in this chapter focus on boosting student and parent participation and proceed from the following key questions:

1. What is the most powerful way to "hook" both students and parents?

2. How do you minimize student and parent anxiety and increase their willingness to share their skills?

3. What do you do when students and parents have become disengaged from the school community?

The Most Powerful Way to "Hook" Students and Parents

Perhaps the best way to engage others is to provide them with opportunities to show themselves at their best. There are a variety of ways in which people are naturally able. They can be naturally articulate, graceful, charismatic, intuitive, or curious—just to name a few. Inviting students to use their natural abilities in the classroom engages them at a higher level and increases their understanding of the subject matter. Inviting parents to do the same, and seeing how they respond, gives you a better idea of the kinds of activities they will embrace and the kinds that they will ignore. It's by fine-tuning your understanding of both your students and their parents that you will be able to advocate for their engagement in a more effective manner. In other words, knowing who they are is key to showing them what other roles they could fill within your learning community.

Multiple Intelligences = Multiple Means

Sometimes when you plan a lesson, you just know that your students will love it and will learn the material easily. You've probably intuited a sense of your students' interests, strengths, and learning styles, and you know how to factor these into your instruction and make it engaging. One way to formalize your intuition is to back it up with data that will give you a clearer picture of what motivates and inspires your students. Howard Gardner (1993) identified eight intelligence types: verbal-linguistic, logical-mathematical, spatial, bodily-kinesthetic, musical, interpersonal, intrapersonal, and naturalist. Attending to multiple types of intelligence encourages students to use their natural talents to achieve understanding in and out of the classroom.

Teachers do this every day. A chemistry teacher might hook the mathematicians and hands-on learners in her class with a lab focused on making silly putty from glue and other household ingredients. A 3rd grade teacher might hook strong readers by teaching German words learned as a child living on an American army base in Germany. A 6th grade teacher might hook competitive students by challenging them to compete against their classmates for the title of top math student. Here are some guidelines for working with the theory of multiple intelligences to engage students.

▶ Expand instruction to address all kinds of learning styles

The teaching style of a traditional classroom is a good fit for students with verbal-linguistic and logical-mathematical intelligences, and it's these students who are traditionally high achievers. However, McArdle, Numrich, and Walsh (2002) report that even though verbal-linguistic intelligence is the mode commonly taught to in schools today, when students in a study were given a choice of assignments reflecting different intelligences, only 12 percent chose a verbal-linguistic one. They noted that "when the students began to recognize their areas of strengths and chose the learning styles that suited them best, observations of student interest and enthusiasm increased significantly. Based on projects presented by students, greater comprehension of material covered was evident" (p. 65). Teachers who adapt their teaching style to the learning styles of the students in their classes will give their students the feeling of being capable in the classroom.

▶ Assess for intelligences

Finding out the types of intelligences preferred by the students sitting in your classroom has the potential for both complicating and simplifying your lesson preparation. It is probable that you will find all eight types represented in your classroom. Many students will display a dominant intelligence, and most will exhibit varying levels of the others. This doesn't mean you'll need to create lessons to appeal to all eight types, however. The wisest approach is to target the majority of your instruction to the two or three intelligences dominant in your classroom, and provide specific activities to draw in the other intelligences along the way. This gives you the best chance of inspiring the greatest number of your students to be the best version of themselves as learners.

Begin incorporating various learning styles into your lessons by using a test to assess students' intelligences. Your school counselor might have access to one or you can ask your parent-teacher organization to fund the Multiple Intelligence Developmental Assessment Scales Program created by C. Branton Shearer for students in grades K–12 (see www.miresearch.org for further information). If you don't have access to test instruments, you can use your intuitive skills to deduce your students' preferred intelligences and adjust your instruction accordingly.

Successful teachers create lessons that most students will learn from. They vary their delivery and their activities to reach students of every type of intelligence, whether that means teaching math facts while doing jumping jacks (bodily-kinesthetic intelligence) or taking the class outside for a hike to learn about biology (naturalist intelligence). This instructional variety communicates to students that each of them is unique in the way they integrate new information into their base of understanding. The more students feel understood, the more easily they let their guard down and try new ideas.

Giving Parents the Power (but Also Preparing Supports)

Convincing parents to commit to engaging in learning activities at school and at home can be a tricky undertaking. You don't want them to think that if they don't volunteer, you will think poorly of them or their children. You do, however, want parents who are unsure about getting involved to understand that just by being a parent, they have something worthwhile to contribute—themselves, their interests, and their abilities. When they make that contribution, their child will benefit. Your invitation to become involved is really an invitation to parents to redefine how they will become further involved in their child's education.

Scaffold the engagement process for parents. The chaperone parent can be pushed to become a "lunch buddy," and the room mom can be encouraged to join the school leadership team. In essence, no matter what grade level you teach and no matter how engaged a parent already is, each year you are asking parents to begin again to support their child's education in a new way. As Brendan Kennelly (2004) writes in his poem "Begin,"

> Though we live in a world that dreams of ending
> that always seems about to give in
> something that will not acknowledge conclusion
> insists that we forever begin.

▶ Issue invitations that build community

Your intention to invite parent engagement must be clear in your mind for it to be clear in parents' minds. My oldest son's kindergarten teacher, Ms. Lawrence, was masterful at motivating parents to participate in school. Throughout the school year, she would instruct her students to design invitations for parents to join the class for a reading tea or an in-class lunch and lesson. The students knew that their parents were invited, and the teacher was sure to send the invitations home in plenty of time for parents to arrange child care for younger siblings. The combination of student enthusiasm and lead time made it difficult for any parent to say no.

Ms. Lawrence gave each parent many opportunities throughout the year to join her in the classroom, facilitating a feeling of welcome for us. Learning how the classroom worked gave us an insight into the rules and expectations that brought about positive behavior choices in our children. We could then use these rules and

---

Source: From *Familiar Strangers: New and Selected Poems 1960–2004* (p. 478) by Brendan Kennelly. Tarset, Northumberland, UK. Copyright 2004 by Bloodaxe Books. Reprinted with permission.

expectations at home, creating congruency for the students as they moved between home and school.

▶ Hold a Parent Day

Teachers of all grades can initiate an opportunity for parents to see the school as a place they want to be. Hold an annual Parent Day where you invite parents to come and spend the day or a part of the day with their child attending classes, student assemblies, and lunch. Put the children in charge, making them responsible for informing their parents when it is appropriate to talk or walk. In the classroom, have students lead a lesson, and assign parents and students a project to complete together. Everyone benefits as the parents reverse roles with their children. During this day, you can highlight engagement opportunities for the parents. With their children looking on and encouraging them, the parents will have a difficult time saying no.

▶ Include noncustodial parents

Invitations that go home in a child's backpack or are sent to the parent who filled out your beginning-of-the-year questionnaire may never reach the parent who has custody every other weekend. Do your best to include all parents who are in a student's life in your classroom community by making a continued effort to include noncustodial parents on your e-mail and text lists, and taking the extra effort to mail your classroom newsletter and any other invitation that the noncustodial parent might miss. The more people a child has rooting for him or her, the better—and noncustodial parents (often fathers) are a valuable resource. A study published by the National Center for Education (Nord, Brimholl, & West, 1997) found that, while noncustodial fathers are less likely to participate at school than custodial fathers, when they are involved, they make a difference, particularly for children in grades 6 and above. Their children are much more likely to get *A*s, report enjoying school, and participate in extracurricular activities, and they are less likely to repeat a grade.

Research has found three important dimensions of father involvement that teachers can focus on to increase a child's academic achievement:

1. *Engagement*—a father's experience of direct contact and shared interactions with his child in the form of caretaking, play, or leisure.

2. *Accessibility*—a father's presence and availability to the child, irrespective of the nature or extent of interactions between father and child.

3. *Responsibility*—a father's understanding and meeting of his child's needs, including the provision of economic resources to the child, and the planning and organizing of children's lives. (Tamis-LeMonda & Cabrera, 1999, p. 6)

Whether the noncustodial parent is a child's mother or father has no bearing on the impact that parent engagement has on a child.

Ideas for Increasing Noncustodial Parents' Engagement

• Offer workshops that suggest developmentally appropriate activities that they can do with their child.

• Directly ask noncustodial parents what they need from the school to help them connect with their child.

• Specifically invite noncustodial parents to participate in activities geared to their skills and interests, such as coming in and presenting on career day.

Ideas for Increasing Noncustodial Parents' Accessibility

• Ensure that noncustodial parents feel welcome to be engaged in their child's school life by consistently inviting them to attend school functions and serve as field trip chaperones.

• Provide suggestions to overcome physical distances between noncustodial parents and their children. For example, students can use the Internet to connect with their parent to ask for help with writing assignments, using guidelines the teacher can send as an e-mail. Students and noncustodial parents can also be encouraged to play online interactive games that promote academic thinking, such as chess and problem solving.

Ideas for Increasing Noncustodial Parents' Responsibility

• Mail or e-mail information about study skills and the importance of providing a homework spot in their home.

• Send noncustodial parents information highlighting the child's skills and challenges, along with suggestions on how to strengthen and attend to both.

How to Minimize Anxiety and Increase a Willingness to Share

Sometimes students fixate on one subject as being troublesome to the extent that they develop an anxiety about the subject. Providing strategies for overcoming this barrier can be pivotal to students whose performance is diminished by anxiety.

If you take the time to explicitly ask them about their interests and abilities, most parents will be happy to tell you. Incorporating their talents into your lesson planning has the potential to help a parent feel capable in the school environment. Parents who weren't successful students themselves or who might not feel successful as adults might feel anxious about becoming involved in the classroom. Address this concern head on by seeking clues to parent interests, preparing clear instructions, and showing your appreciation for all parent engagement. These are surefire ways to change some parents' outlook.

Reducing Student Anxiety

The Hebrew sage Hillel advised that "a person too anxious about being shamed cannot learn." Student anxiety is deleterious to student achievement and can lead to displays of out-of-character signs of frustration (including misbehavior and other negative behavior). You can take steps to seek out the source of the problem and resolve it—sometimes in private, sometimes in class, but always with the focus of inquiry squarely on addressing the learning struggle rather than the student's behavior.

▶ Focus more on understanding than on "right" or "wrong"

Before students even have a chance to become frustrated, be mindful of the potential sticking points of a lesson. Students often develop feelings of anxiety and frustration when they don't understand an idea. All too often, the perceived difficulty of a problem sidetracks students and keeps them from considering the full range of solution options. One critical way of heading off these negative emotions is to present problems and their solutions in more than one way. By encouraging students to think of the various ways to approach a challenging task and the various ways they might reach a solution, you help them worry less about being wrong (that is, looking dumb in front of their peers) and concentrate more on understanding how they arrived at their answer.

▶ Check for understanding

Formative assessment—taking regular formal and informal measurements of student progress toward learning objectives—allows you to gauge student anxiety levels and adjust your instructional approaches accordingly. Not only does this practice alert you to students who might be so anxious about the work involved in completing an assignment that they quit halfway through, it also helps you find the most effective motivational means to bring your students to a higher level of understanding.

▶ Reframe supplemental lessons in a positive way

When students need extra help mastering objectives, introduce supplemental lessons as "new strategies" to encourage them to try a difficult concept again. These additional strategies can give your struggling students another go at a difficult concept in a way that reduces the pressure they might feel about being "the kid who needs remediation." Spinning additional work as an alternate strategy helps them save face and gives them a chance to prove to themselves and to you that they can learn whatever you are teaching.

▶ Teach students a new way to look at intelligence

Help your students see that they are master and commander of their learning selves. If they believe that they are incapable, they are right; if they believe they are smart, they are right, too. Stress that intelligence is an aspect of themselves that can change—not something they are stuck with or slowed down by. Bempechat, London, and Dweck (1991) found that when children view intelligence as a flexible reflection of their ability, they tend to describe intelligence in others on the basis of the actions the other students take to become smarter. They say things like "He's smart because he always does his homework" or "She's smart because she always tries her hardest." These children display an understanding that learning is a process, one that allows them to increase both their skills and their knowledge. For children who orient their thinking in this way, worries about how smart they are relative to others are not a factor in how well they do in school. They tend not to get anxious about learning something new because they have the tools that help them break a new topic into understandable parts.

Reducing Parent Anxiety

Information—flowing both from the parent to you and from you to the parent—is your main ally in making parents more comfortable. Matching parents' skill sets to volunteer opportunities is an important first step. However, because parents aren't in the school environment as often as you are, they will likely need help connecting the skills they have to offer with the volunteer opportunities available. Figure 6.1 provides some quick guidelines to get you started.

Figure 6.1

Suggested Pairings of Parent Skills and Engagement Opportunities

Parent Skill	Engagement Opportunity
Advising people	Partner with students as they plan out a project
Analyzing data	Work on leadership team to distill test scores into goals for school administration, teachers, and parents
Checking for accuracy	Edit the class newsletter
Coaching	Lead a sport or activity that isn't currently offered, such as chess or soccer
Community organization/ involvement/volunteerism	Recruit community volunteers and establish community partnerships
Construction/landscaping	Build props for school play or help with school landscape
Creating charts and slideshow presentations	Create a visual presentation to heighten student understanding
Creating visual displays/ scrapbooking	Help set up student art shows
Finding information	Research titles of new age-appropriate reading material
Handling numerical data	Maintain records for student group to help students understand income and expenses
Meeting new people	Organize coffee mornings or dinners out for parents
Organization	Help disorganized students clean out their lockers or desks, placing loose papers into the appropriate binders and putting items in piles for home, class, or the library
Planning and time management	Assist in setting and sticking to an agenda during a student club meeting

Parent Skill	Engagement Opportunity
Promotion/public relation skills	Head up publicity campaigns focused on school programs and events
Public speaking	Represent the school in district events for students and parents
Speaking a second language	Translate class newsletter or website for nonnative students and parents
Summarizing information	Provide a summary of school board meetings for school community`
Teaching	Work with struggling students in a small group or one on one
Updating/managing files	Sort student work into appropriate folders
Writing/editing	Summarize student trips and school activities for the school newsletter, website, or the local newspaper
Writing for publication	Give a presentation on how to ready a manuscript for publication

Taking the time to connect parent skills to needs in your classroom or the school at large will be seen as another act of consideration that will serve you well as you work to engage parents in the process of their children's education.

▶ Look for clues to parent interests

People feel comfortable completing tasks that they are familiar with and understand the directions for. Take the time to meet these needs and parents will be much more comfortable volunteering their time and energy in and out of your classroom. Students can give you insight into what their parents are interested in if you take the time to listen and look for some telltale clues like the following:

• If you see homemade cookies in a student's lunchbox every day, during a unit on chemical processes, you might invite the parent to come in and demonstrate how to make cookies while you explain the science involved.

• If a student talks about how much interest he is earning from his savings account during a study of how to figure percentages, invite the parent in to explain how savings accounts function.

• If every Monday a student comes in with a full account of the movie she watched with her dad over the weekend, invite the parent to edit for sensory details in student stories or ask if that parent would be willing to burn DVDs of educational programs.

▶ Create job descriptions for recurring jobs and offer training

Everybody feels better about completing a task that they understand. Consider creating job descriptions for parents for those jobs that involve a number of steps and giving them to parents when they first sign up for the task. The visual reinforcement as well as your verbal explanation the first time they learn about the job will facilitate their understanding. It also gives them a reference if they happen to forget a step once they begin.

Parent volunteers always benefit from having a clear sense of what is expected of them. In my parent training, I include general information such as a map of the school, along with suggestions on how to interact with the students. I like to tell my parent volunteers that it's OK for them to "dare to care" about their child's classmates. I've encouraged them to high-five the students, engage in discussions that don't have anything to do with our content, and compliment students' fashion choices.

I also create a list of "do's and don'ts" covering topics that range from working with the students, to the dress code, to general expectations. Keep this list simple. An example follows:

Do...
• Find out what I want you to work on.
• Learn the students' names.
• Encourage all students.

- Share any concerns with me.
- Be friendly but firm with the students.
- Keep details about student performance and behavior confidential.
- Enjoy yourself!

Don't...
- Arrive late. Help us stay on schedule and make everyone's day happy.
- Start the activity until you understand the objectives.
- Be afraid to tell me a concern about the lesson or a student.

Thank you for your time, energy, and commitment to education!

When putting together trainings or guidelines for parent volunteers, the best advice is to try to see the situation from the parents' point of view. When they show up, you want them to have everything they need to successfully complete their task. Be sure to introduce them to the personnel that they will be interacting with, prepare materials in advance (with written directions), and break big jobs into smaller tasks.

What to Do When Students and Parents Become Disengaged

From time to time, most students will find themselves just taking up space in the classroom; they need a hook to help them regain their interest in learning. If you regularly address this issue—and even discuss it with your students—you can ensure that when anyone does disengage, it's only a temporary thing.

Parents have the advantage over students in that they aren't legally bound to arrive at school each morning. They have obligations that demand their attention, and they can easily shroud reluctance about involvement with the excuse "I don't have the time."

If you're prepared to hear this from parents, you can be ready with responses that give them easy ways to engage on their own terms.

Engaging the Disengaged Student

Getting students to think and share what they are thinking is a significant goal for a teacher, but students are often reluctant to do this. Rather than jump into the "think tank" and swim, they remain on the side and just dip in their toes.

Think of academics as a neutral ground for students. They might be going through a personal problem that prevents them from fully engaging in the classroom. If you can figure out appropriate motivators, classwork can serve as a means of escape from their troubles because the subject matter doesn't have to have anything to do with them. In addition, if you use interpersonal strategies to engage your students in learning, they will learn to involve their personalities in their learning, engaging them further in the learning process. They learn not only your lesson but also how to cope with a personal problem. Use these strategies for the whole class, and all of your students will benefit.

▶ Address disengagement head on

Begin a discussion about those moments when learners feel stuck during a lesson. Write a few of these fear-related questions on the board:

- Am I the only one who doesn't "get" this?
- Is frustration normal?
- Why is it so hard to pay attention?
- Why do I need to know this anyway?
- Am I just plain dumb?

Let your students know that it is normal to want to avoid the bad feelings these kinds of fears cause; that is why they might find themselves procrastinating or even cleaning their room when they really "should" be doing their homework or studying for an exam. It is also normal to feel nervous, get a stomachache, or wonder about how smart they are when they're faced with a difficult task. Teach your students to tune in to how their body responds to stress, accept it, and keep going.

When students are facing a difficult task, many of them are tempted to disengage from the task altogether. Teach them to silently ask self-regulating questions to assess their desire to quit, so they can get back on track. For example, you might encourage them to ask themselves these questions:

- What part of this is frustrating me?
- What can I do to "get" this?
- If I take a break, how long will it be?

The answers to these questions will help them create a plan and get them back on track to learning.

Kids don't own much. Their main commodities are their pride, their intelligence, their appearance, and their sense of humor. When working with a disengaged student, start with what they own, and move forward from there.

Addressing the Issue of Parents Who Demur or Drop Out

You will always have a few parents who might express interest in being involved or show up for one volunteer activity but then cancel commitments or otherwise withdraw from the classroom community. Instead of shrugging off this "dropping out" as inevitable and moving on to the next parent, develop a plan. There are a number of strategies to consider—some reactive and some proactive.

▶ Suggest new (and even unconventional) kinds of involvement

Parents' actions and their demurrals when you invite them to become engaged can provide valuable insight into the kinds of activities they might be willing to engage in—ones they didn't know existed or didn't see as fitting the definition of "parent involvement."

Here are some guidelines that might help parents to think outside the box regarding involvement in the school.

Ideas for the Parents Who "Have No Time"

• Suggest "just because" activities to help parents make the most of their free time with their child. These will vary with the ages of the student, but here are a range of examples:

* Play a quick game of Go Fish or War.
* Take a walk in the rain.
* Race each other on bikes.
* Draw on the sidewalk with chalk.
* Ask for the child's advice on a new car.
* Bring the child to the store to help pick out new paint for the house.
* Picnic in the backyard.
* Attend a yoga, dance, or drama class together.

• Ask if parents can complete volunteer tasks at home or after school, and have a task organized to hand over right then. Examples might include the following:

* Cut out and collate student projects.
* Staple sheets of practice exercises.
* Write thank-you notes to local businesses who support the school.
* Develop school photos, given a memory card and a reimbursement form.

▶ Show your appreciation for parent volunteers

A small gesture of thanks will go a long way in showing your appreciation to parents and encouraging them to volunteer in the future. Ideas to consider include thank-you notes, e-mails, texts, and phone calls; small gifts; certificates of achievement; recognition in a class newsletters, school assemblies, and board meetings; and volunteer luncheons.

Another key way to show your appreciation is to ask parents who have volunteered or participated in at-home supportive activities to give you feedback about their experience. Always listen carefully to any concerns they have, and follow up appropriately and in a timely manner.

▶ Create a parent volunteer database

It is temptingly easy to ask the same enthusiastic parents to pitch in whenever a need arises, but doing so shortchanges the rest of your potential parent volunteer pool—and denies some students the benefits associated with having an engaged parent. Setting up a simple database with contact details, notes about skills and interests, and a record of past participation helps ensure you can mix things up and find the right volunteers for the jobs you have.

▶ Be adaptable

Be sure to update your volunteer activities as the skills and needs of your parents change from year to year. One year parents might need help with parenting skills; the next, they might be interested in creating a school garden. Both are valid forms of parent engagement. Embrace the different ways parents can funnel their energy into the school environment.

Masks Down, Meaningful Engagement Up

Effective teachers want students and parents to become so swept up in their school engagement experiences that they forget to wear their usual masks, be they cool, dorky, shy, or academic. Work toward an atmosphere of welcome, so parents and students alike can enthusiastically participate in a meaningful way. In doing so, you will expand the learning community and foster the kind of success that is built on the participation of each student and each parent.

Engagement Challenges

There are challenges in every relationship, and teacher-student and teacher-parent relationships are no exception. Effective teachers regard these challenges as a means of forging deeper, richer, and more trusting connection with all parties. This trust works to counteract negative feelings that students and parents might associate with school and helps point them in the direction of achievement.

Successful teachers know to anticipate setbacks related to reaching and connecting with both students and parents. They create plans that fit current patterns of parent and student need and clarify roles and responsibilities for themselves, students, and parents. In Chapters 7 and 8, we look at how to prepare for and ultimately benefit from the challenges of student and parent engagement. It's a matter of creating effective learning opportunities and reframing perspectives in a manner that appreciates and stretches current skills.

7

Creating More Effective Learning Opportunities

> Out beyond ideas of Wrongdoing and Rightdoing, there is a field. I'll meet you there. When the soul lies down in that grass, the world is too full to talk about. Ideas, language, and even the phrase "each other" doesn't make any sense.
>
> ✻ RUMI, C. 532 CE ✻

Educators all over the world are searching for that one perfect practice that is going to revolutionize the school experience. I haven't discovered that perfect practice yet, but I have found an assortment of good practices to initiate, modify, and implement year after year.

Instruction that leads students to achieve goals and meet standards is built on a solid foundation and evolves throughout the school year. For teachers, it is less a matter of "wrongdoing" or "rightdoing" than of simply doing. The key is to focus on your students' needs. This is a never-ending but enormously rewarding process.

In this chapter, we'll look at how to create learning opportunities by removing common barriers and ensuring proper support. Here are the questions we will focus on:

1. How do you cultivate a strong, focused work ethic in your students and get parent support for these efforts?

2. How do you assess and utilize students' and parents' interpersonal skills to boost success and engagement?

How to Cultivate a Work Ethic and Gain Parent Support for This Effort

After working to create engagement opportunities and then advertising these opportunities to students and parents, your next step is to tout hard work as the necessary means to student achievement. In the world students are growing up in, so much can be acquired so quickly—with a click of a mouse, a swipe of a card, or tap of a keystroke—that honest to goodness hard work and extended effort can seem pretty daunting. Hard work is hard, yes, but it is rewarding, as students realize when they experience it themselves. Teach them the steps, and seek parent support for this effort by communicating it as a goal, inviting contributions, and providing tools for parents to use to provide at-home reinforcement.

Focusing Students on Tools for Today *and* Tomorrow

What teachers know—but students don't always—is that positive academic and behavioral habits have both immediate and long-range benefits. Most students want to make good choices, but part of being young is sometimes struggling with what defines a choice as "good" or "bad." Teachers have a valuable role to play as guides and models; we can help our students understand and favor positive choices and steer away from negative ones. Modeling the behavior we want to see can be an effective strategy.

▶ **Stress the connection between working hard and learning**

Knowing that hard work leads to learning is an essential understanding, and the way you present the idea to students has a lot to do with how well they will internalize it. The key is to emphasize both how they will benefit from undertaking a task or mastering a goal and the behaviors that will help them do so. Good and Brophy (2000) note that when effective teachers introduce an activity, they stress the activity's purpose, or what students will learn from it. These teachers also treat making mistakes and working with classmates as natural parts of the learning process. Both tactics encourage students to ask questions without embarrassment, contribute to lessons without fear of their ideas being ridiculed, and collaborate with one another on many of their learning activities. In other words, when teachers focus on the purpose of an academic task and the skills and behaviors that help students achieve it, it's more likely that students will understand that achievement is more a matter of effort than of natural talent. And when it comes to putting forth the effort, there are reliable processes they can follow and supports they can turn to.

▶ Dangle an attractive carrot

During his first year of teaching, Mr. Yost, a former colleague of mine, found that classroom management problems in his high school English class were derailing everyone's learning. He decided to put students in charge of their own behavior by developing a discipline incentive plan, or DIP. The plan involved inviting well-behaved students to attend a play with him on a weekend. The students would receive substantial extra credit for attending the play and submitting a written one-page summary or critique. Nobody with a discipline problem would be allowed to go, he explained to his students; however, each quarter, he would wipe the discipline slate clean.

This approach proved very effective, and the DIP program is still going strong in his classroom. For some students, this is the first "cultural event" they have ever attended. And after the play, Mr. Yost always initiates casual, intelligent discussion of theater with his students. The idea, he explains, is to nudge the kids toward identifying with positive, thoughtful, well-mannered, adult behaviors.

What was a response to problems in his classes is also a tool he uses to help students take control of their behavioral choices and help them reach for something they didn't even know they wanted.

▶ Add positive words to your everyday discourse

Effective teachers enhance learning by incorporating positive, respectful language into their everyday discussions with students (Wang et al., 2008). Using respectful language such as "Yes, sir" or "Go on, madam" with students models how you would like to be addressed and illustrates the respect you have for your students. Addressing middle and high school students as "Mr. Jones" or "Ms. Turner" is also a respectful nod toward their future adult self. I've referred to my future lawyers as "Attorney General," future doctors as "Doc," and writers as "Mr. Hemingway" or "Ms. Woolf." These positive monikers urge students to break through limits they may have placed on themselves.

Mary Phillips Manke (1997) suggests that employing such politeness is an effective means of sharing power with students. She explains that in place of commands in the classroom, teachers can ask students questions ("Would you please come take your seat, Manuel?") or make statements of preference ("Manuel, I would really like for you take your seat."). Using the modals "would" and "could" effectively softens a teacher's request, making it more palatable for the student. She also recommends that requests incorporate the use of "please," "thank you," and "excuse me."

Focusing Parents on Their Homework Role

When you assign homework and collect it each day, you are relying on 30 kids and their parents to have the discipline and organizational skills to complete the assigned exercises. Parents can be your biggest supporters—if you imbue in them the belief that the homework you give has a real purpose. Make it explicit that the homework you assign is *not* busywork, and that by completing homework, their child will make progress in your class. There are several supports you can put in place to help achieve this end.

▶ Develop and share a homework philosophy

I recommend taking the time to develop and publicize a homework philosophy that appeals to the wants and needs of all parents and includes a description of how you plan homework assignments with each child in mind. When you develop your homework philosophy, envision it as the underpinning of your classroom practice. It's also something you'll have to be able to defend, so be sure to develop one that reflects your goals and values.

Questions to Consider When Developing a Homework Philosophy

1. *What do you believe to be the purpose of homework?* Do the assignments provide extra practice, prepare students for an upcoming lesson, extend in-class learning, or give students a chance to exercise their creativity?

2. *How much time do you believe homework assignments should require?* A common guideline is to give 10 minutes of homework per grade level each night.

3. *How will you review the assignments?* Will you check homework personally, or will you check homework in class as a form of peer coaching?

4. *How will you grade the assignments?* How much will homework count for in a student's grade? Will students be graded on the correctness of their work or on the fact that it is completed and turned in?

5. *How should parents be involved?* Should parents correct homework? Sign it to acknowledge their child did it on his or her own?

▶ Give parents clear guidelines for helping with homework

Offering guidelines helps to build parents' trust that you have thought through your homework assignments and tied them to curricular goals. As the example handout in Figure 7.1 shows, I think it is important to provide my students' parents with very explicit information about homework, including the *what* and the *why*.

Parents who understand how to be involved effectively with their child's homework and how vital this involvement is are more likely to provide sustained support throughout the school year. Many parents have told me that they find homework time to be a stressful time that they would rather avoid. A 1999 report issued by Public Agenda characterizes homework as a "nightly dilemma," with 50 percent of parents surveyed having had "serious arguments with their child over assignments" to the point that there was "yelling or crying" (Farkas, Johnson, & Duffett, 1999, para. 11). In focus groups, many parents questioned the value of homework and viewed a child's ability to complete homework without supervision as the mark of an independent child.

Providing parents with your homework rationale helps counter this skepticism, as does ensuring that there are clear, jargon-free, step-by-step directions for each assignment you send home. This practice will help parents know how to begin when their frustrated child needs assistance or when they simply want to understand the task their child is working on. In addition, your class website can provide specific directions for all assignments or particular ones, along with general directions for assisting students at home.

The purpose behind this detailed guidance is to help change homework from a roadblock to an opportunity—a chance for parents and children to connect and for parents to understand their child's world. It also provides a means for parents to encourage children's image of themselves as learners and capable students.

▶ Stress parents' power to support academic achievement

Research confirms the benefits of parental involvement in children's homework. For example, Siraj-Blatchford, Sylva, Muttock, Gilden, and Bell (2002) found that parental involvement in learning activities at home shows a close association with better cognitive attainment in the early years. Research by Catsambis (2001)

Figure 7.1

Sample Parent Handout: Homework Philosophy and Guidelines

Parent Help at Homework Time Improves Student Learning

You know your child best. With your assistance during homework time, your child will gain necessary skills along with the confidence that will support success in school.

My Philosophy

I give homework for one of four reasons:
1. To provide practice time for students to master what I've taught them.
2. To prepare students for upcoming lessons.
3. To give students a chance to work with a skill in a new way.
4. To showcase the spectrum of skills the students have gained.

Frequency of Homework Assignments

Most nights, students will have homework from my class. As 10th graders, they have 4 core subjects per day and are capable of 100 minutes of homework per night. Students should expect approximately 25 minutes of homework in each subject.

How to Help

- Develop a homework routine and stick to it.
- Provide a quiet, well-lit study area stocked with pencils, pens, paper, and a dictionary.
- Be available for encouragement and clarification.
- Look over the assignment for completeness and neatness.
- Talk about what your child is learning.

When There Is a Problem

Please contact me if you experience any of the following:
- Your child is regularly taking much longer than 25 minutes to finish the homework I have assigned.
- You feel that your child requires too much supervision and explanation during homework time.
- Homework is becoming a source of conflict between you and your child.

involving 14- to 18-year-olds concluded that high levels of parental expectation, consistent encouragement, and actions to enhance learning opportunities in the home were all positively associated with students' high aspirations and college enrollment regardless of the students' socioeconomic status or ethnic background. Involving parents in homework is a worthwhile pursuit, as it can reach every parent—even the ones who can't or won't become involved on the actual school grounds.

Homework can prove to be a chrysalis within which students can nurture the life skills they will need as adults. Mel Levine points out in *The Myth of Laziness* (2003) that homework is "a means to bolster some of the most important components of high-quality output, such as the capacity to sustain mental effort, the ability to prepare for an important upcoming event, the proficiency to organize materials and one's own thinking, the organizational insight to know how to manage time and meet deadlines, and the sense of producing independently outside the structure of a classroom" (p. 150).

The parent's role in this effort is a tricky one to manage. Children can "read" adult reactions to school-related habits and grades and deduce an estimation of their own ability. For example, if parents stop trying to help their child when the child doesn't seem to be making progress, the child may internalize the idea that she is not worthy of her mom and dad's help. She might even come to believe that she is a failure and accept that label as her identity. Alternatively, when a parent sits with a child and helps him with every homework problem, the student might come to believe that he is incapable of completing assignments on his own. Both of these negative beliefs have the tendency to steer students toward lower academic performance. In fact, research has shown that high-achieving students place more stock in a parent's belief about their ability than in the evidence of ability depicted on their report cards (Phillips, 1987).

When parents are aware of how their perceptions, actions, and reactions can affect their child, they can go about changing their responses to their child's academic performance. You might start by giving them ideas for activities they can do together in which the child can be successful and show the parent how able he or she is. These activities can be fun and, at the same time, develop skills that are transferable to school, such as math proficiency, strategy, and independent thinking. A teacher of young children might steer parents toward board games that encourage these skills like Monopoly, Chutes and Ladders, Yahtzee, Uno, and Crazy Eights. Middle and high school teachers might look to any number of hobby books, newspapers, and catalogs parents could use in home learning activities. In her book *MegaSkills,* Dorothy Rich (2008) suggests hundreds of activities to help parents and students work together to grow the behaviors and skills students will need to be successful in school, such as communicating using notes for five minutes, practicing fractions by folding a paper towel, or writing a joint parent-child letter to the local newspaper on a topic that is relevant to families.

It can't hurt to ask parents to drill the skills that students need to know automatically, such as math facts and grammar rules. If a student is stopping to figure out the answer to 6×3, then solving 486×53 will be an exercise in frustration. Ingraining these rote skills into students' minds provides a strong base of understanding, freeing mental space to take on more difficult problems. If parents commit to running through a set of math flash cards once a night, they will quickly see the impact of their involvement.

▶ Assign homework that requires parent participation

Give parents the chance to share their experiences and explore new ones with their children by assigning interactive homework assignments. These assignments legitimize a parent's involvement for the student because the parent participation is *required.* Bempechat (1998) notes that "unsolicited help from an adult can be interpreted [by children] as an indication of low ability"; when parents start helping before children ask for help, children "conclude that they must not be smart, since the adult in question felt the need to offer assistance" (p. 47). Giving assignments that explicitly call for parental involvement shows students that their parents are needed, and it is OK for them to become involved.

These assignments also make families aware of the topics that students are studying and the students' responses to the topic. They give students an opportunity to discuss ideas at home, and they give teachers another means to communicate with families about school news, class news, curriculum, and homework. Interactive homework assignments tend to shift the focus from the product of learning to the process of learning, because they encourage students to temporarily forget the negative beliefs they hold about themselves as they enjoy themselves with their parents. Finally, these assignments offer built-in guidance for how parents can help their children. Dauber and Epstein (1993) found in their research that it was this type of guidance that parents of both elementary and middle school children reported needing in order to help their children more.

When it comes to designing interactive homework assignments, I recommend using the Teachers Involve Parents in Schoolwork (TIPS) template created by Epstein and colleagues (2009). The TIPS templates include a welcome message to families, a statement of the assignment objectives, the materials needed, directions for task completion, a home-to-school communication, and a place for a parent signature. Figure 7.2 shows a sample TIPS interactive homework assignment that parents, teachers, administrators, and I developed together. Epstein and her team have designed many TIPS assignments for science, language arts, and math, and templates for each subject area are available on the TIPS website: www.csos.jhu.edu/P2000/tips/index.htm

The tools you give parents to use while helping their children with homework will extend beyond that one assignment; they offer ways for parents to interact with their children all of the time. Parents might learn to ask their children questions instead of simply giving away answers. They might become more interested in hearing their children's point of view. They might come to believe they

Figure 7.2
A TIPS Writing Assignment

Student's Name: _____ Date: _____

Forget the Sky, Chicken Little. *We* Are Falling!

Dear Family Partner:

We are learning how to imagine a situation and write a story about it. For this assignment, we are going to imagine together so that we can collect ideas for a story. I need your help to describe details and explain meanings that will make the story interesting. I hope you enjoy doing this activity with me. This assignment is due _____.

Sincerely,

_____
(Student's signature)

IMAGINING TOGETHER

Imagine that you just woke up and realized that you are a raindrop. You see yourself falling toward the earth below you. Clouds are swirling above you. Write a story about what you and your family of raindrops decide to do once you hit the ground.

Find a Family Member to Imagine With
1. Invite a family member to be a raindrop with you. Who is it? _____
2. Read the writing prompt out loud.
3. Answer these questions:

- What does it feel like to be a raindrop?
- What makes you a special raindrop?
- What can you as an imaginary raindrop do on the ground?
- What do you want to do once you land?
- How did you feel when you were a raindrop? Scared? Excited?
- What does this story say about you as a family?

First Draft
Use the information from your interview to respond to the writing prompt.
Remember to

- Give your story a title.
- Write a sentence that tells the reader what you are going to write about.
- Be sure all of your sentences relate to your topic.
- Use descriptive words to help explain the ideas, and use "I," "me," and "my" as you tell the story.

Write your story title and craft a paragraph.

Read your paragraph twice with your family partner. First, read it as readers (imagine the story) and then read it as writers (analyze the writing). Revise or add sentences as needed.

Extension Activity
Select another object to pretend to be—for example, a kitchen table, a birthday present, a dog, or anything else that interests you. What object did you choose? Next to each "Q" line below, write a question about your topic. Ask your family member to interview you, using your questions. Ask your family member to write your answer next to each "A" line.

1. Q:
   A:
2. Q:
   A:
3: Q:
   A:
4: Q:
   A:

Home-to-School Connection
Dear Parent/Guardian,
Your comments about your child's work on this activity are important.
Please write YES or NO for each statement:
___ My child understood this homework assignment and was able to discuss it.
___ My child and I enjoyed this activity.
___ This assignment helps me understand what my child is learning about writing.
___ I feel capable of helping my child with homework and helping him or her identify as a writer.

Other comments:

Parent/Guardian signature: _____

can make a difference instead of thinking their children's school lives and home lives are two different entities.

How to Assess and Utilize Students' and Parents' Interpersonal Skills to Boost Success and Engagement

Often, when students are struggling to learn, they aren't able to articulate the source of their struggle. They don't know how to tell you, for example, that they don't understand the steps of the math problem or the metaphors used in *The Scarlet Letter*. What they need are interpersonal tools that will help them separate their academic barriers from their emotional ones. Separating out the frustration of not understanding the lesson from a general lack of confidence will help students tell their teacher what they don't understand instead of just throwing up their hands and giving up.

Teaching Students About Their Own Power

Students need to understand that learning is not contingent on their incoming interest in the subject matter; they are indeed capable of completing work in all subject areas. You can convince them of this by sharing tools that will help them help themselves. Share the tools of successful learners to help students enhance their learning, even when the subject matter doesn't interest them.

▶ Engage in regular community-building activity

Cooperation, assertiveness, responsibility, empathy, and self-control do not show up in our collections of academic standards, but they are skills that will help students achieve both inside and outside school; for this reason, they are very much worth a teacher's time and attention. I recommend addressing them during a daily "Morning Meeting." This is a good way to begin the day for elementary classes and a meaningful activity that can fill that often undefined span of time called homeroom in middle and high school classes.

In *The Morning Meeting Book* (2002), Roxann Kriete explains that the Morning Meeting "provides an arena where distinctions that define social, emotional, and academic skills fade, and learning becomes an integrated experience" (p. 15). Begin with a message on a chart near the classroom door to catch students' attention as they enter the classroom. This message could be a welcome, a reminder, or a question. When the Morning Meeting begins, open with a greeting to help students feel a sense of belonging. This greeting evolves over time. In the beginning of the school year, the greeting can be from the teacher to the group, with encouragement from the teacher for each student to greet one another. Each meeting after that, model words and facial expressions that you expect the students to incorporate in their greetings to one another until the students reach a proficient level. Students then move into a sharing portion, when they practice face-to-face conversation. The sharer presents his or her news and, when ready, says, "I am ready for questions or comments." The listeners are then free to make comments or ask questions to demonstrate their interest in the sharer and his or her subject. This gives students a chance to fine-tune their skills in listening, presenting, taking turns, creating questions, and understanding different perspectives.

The Morning Meeting then moves into the group activity, a brief, fast-paced activity involving all members. The activity can involve academic or study skills, or it can just be for fun. A wonderful book chock-full of elementary activity ideas is *99 Activities and Greetings* by Melissa Correa-Connelly (2004). For middle and high school activities, I recommend *Great Group Games* by Susan Ragsdale and Ann Saylor (2007).

To wrap up the Morning Meeting, the students respond to the message on the chart as a means of transitioning into the day's lesson. The meeting should last anywhere from 15 to 30 minutes, and it is an effective means of easing students into their day and preparing them to jump into schoolwork.

▶ Show students how to make themselves interested

It's a nifty trick: by creating the physical approximation of interest, students can actually predispose their minds to embrace new learning. I have found that providing my students with tips for "faking interest" will consistently give them an avenue to make real connections to classroom content.

Ways That Students Can "Fake It 'til They Make It"

• *Lean in toward a speaker.* This promotes the feeling of shared interest. People are always more interested in a topic when they know others are interested in it.

• *Maintain eye contact.* Students will keep their focus on the conversation instead of the clock ticking or students walking down the hall. As students look each other in the eyes, they notice subtle displays of excitement and confusion. This serves to increase interest in the subject.

• *SLANT.* Teachers in KIPP (Knowledge Is Power Program) schools explicitly teach success strategies to the formerly failing students that populate their school. They practice behaviors in their classrooms that help students make classroom participation a habit. Throughout the school day, students are reminded to "SLANT": Sit up, Listen, Ask questions, Nod your head, and Track the speaker with your eyes. The repeated reminders encourage skill automaticity.

▶ Teach gestures that promote learning

When you introduce a lesson, try attaching specific hand gestures to each step of the lesson. Encourage students to repeat the gestures as they practice the steps. This practice helps students create problem-solving strategies expressed through gesture that connects them to material that they had previously not understood (Broaders, Wagner Cook, Mitchell, & Goldin-Meadow, 2007).

A study conducted at the University of Chicago concluded that teaching students gestures positively influenced not just immediate learning but also the students' ability to deduce instructions not made explicitly verbally or through gesture:

> [Children] told to move their hands in a fully correct rendition of a particular problem-solving strategy during a math lesson solved more math problems correctly after the lesson than children told to move their hands in a partially correct rendition of the strategy, who, in turn, solved more problems correctly than children told not to move their hands at all.... Because a grouping strategy was never expressed in speech during the lesson by either child or experimenter, nor was it expressed in gesture by the experimenter, the information that children incorporated into their postlesson speech must have come from their own gestures. The data thus suggest that gesturing can facilitate learning by helping children extract information from their own hand movements. (Goldin-Meadow, Wagner Cook, & Mitchell, 2009, p. 4)

In other words, teaching students gestural problem-solving steps helps them make inferences through a body-mind connection that will, in turn, lead to more enduring learning.

In Buddhist sculpture and art, the Buddha is seen with his hands held in positions that hold specific meaning. These are called mudras. Current-day Japanese monks use these hand positions in their spiritual exercises and worship as a means of relating to the Buddha on wisdoms to overcome five human frailties—wisdom against anger, envy, desire, ignorance, and pride. Creating mudras specific to your class will give your students a connection to content and help them separate the frustration they have with learning the content from the frustration they might be having with learning in general. Gestural expression is an outlet and a tool students can use to improve their understanding, and it is also a great source of formative assessment data when you are seeking to understand your students' academic and affective status.

Ways Students Can Use Gesturing

- *To describe.* Hand motions are an easy way convey different sizes and shapes of both physical and metaphorical things (e.g., small, smaller, and smallest; rectangular, oval, or square; important or not important). They can also indicate direction or position (e.g., horizontal or vertical; backward or forward; near or far).

- *To emphasize.* Students can use gestures to convey their attitude or opinion about a topic, idea, or whatever verbal response they might have (e.g., widening their eyes to express shock, raising a fist to express anger, frowning deeply to express sadness or confusion, crossing their arms to express great frustration).

- *To suggest another meaning.* Extending one's hand is a sign of welcome, and shrugging one's shoulders is a sign of confusion. Students might use gestures like this to send a message they might be uncomfortable expressing verbally.

Keeping Parents in the Skill-Building Loop

You encourage parents to promote positive feelings about academics and school life when you keep them informed by offering clear directions, sharing contact information just in case they have a question, and sending home interactive homework assignments. Assume that all your parents want to support your instructional efforts. Communicating with parents about specific skills you wish to develop will increase the effectiveness of your parental engagement efforts.

▶ Let parents know what you are doing

Share with parents your plans to tap into students' interpersonal skills to boost their academic skills. For example, if you're teaching gestures, parents might rightfully wonder about the point of teaching sign language to their hearing children. Clarify this with a newsletter home about the practice.

▶ **Create mudras that parents can use with their children**

Encourage parents to routinely use gestures when they are speaking to their children. Making a gesture for pouring with their hand while asking, "Would you empty all the garbage cans in the house?" will help a child lock in to the parent's directions. When they tell their child a story, parents can incorporate hand movements to convey emotions such as frustration (a tight fist) or excitement (a splayed hand). In addition, creating hand signals for tense family moments or for when the parent is on the phone will help clarify meaning for both parent and child and help the child understand.

▶ **Share the inside scoop on student interactions**

You are a witness to how your students interact with their peers. When you relay observations about positive and negative student peer interactions to parents, they might respond with incredulity because the behavior you're describing seems out of character. You, on the other hand, see the behavior every day and believe it is the norm for the student.

There's a reason for the great divide—it's called peer influence. Judith Rich Harris (2009) found that "a parent's behavior toward a child affects how the child behaves in the presence of the parent or in contexts that are associated with the parent" (p. 72). When the parent is not around, children will choose behavior that they believe will make them fit in with their school group. Talk frankly with parents about their child's "normal" classroom behavior, and stress that they can extend their own good influence through a presence at school and a support of school at home.

Understanding and Skill Sharing Supports Learning

When students feel that their teacher "gets" them, a powerful connection is made. That is why students refer to these teachers in such life-altering terms as "She saved my life," "He turned me around," and "She saw me for who I really am." Sharing with parents tools that they can use to demonstrate that they also "get" their children can further academic success and provide a model for students' future decision making.

Reframing Perspectives

S uccessful teachers create distinct worlds within their classrooms. These worlds have their own roles, mores, and expectations, and in these worlds, there are possibilities students might not be accustomed to seeing. If the world of your classroom is attractive enough, students will come to accept the habits, value systems, and standards you set and become participating members of your community.

In the same way, you, as a classroom teacher, can help parents to self-identify as active, supporting members of their child's academic life. You are the primary means by which parents will understand that their effort makes a difference—in their own child's achievement and in the achievement of all children in the school. Working to create parent leaders *inside* your classroom is the best way to motivate positive parent engagement *beyond* your classroom walls.

The challenge is to reframe students' and parents' perspectives on what is possible and desirable, and in this chapter, we'll look at strategies for doing that, proceeding from the following questions:

1. How do you convince students and parents to engage at a higher level?

2. How do you maximize the number of students and parents that you target for increased engagement?

3. How can you use negative attitudes as a catalyst for productive change?

Convincing Students and Parents to Engage at a Higher Level

Stacey's eyes were alight when I overheard her in the hall telling a friend how she was studying the influence of hip-hop music on the English language. She said, "Ms. Ridnouer gets me! I never even thought about why we call it 'rap,' but it has to do with the beats in the music." I walked by with a wave and a smile. She pointed at me and said, "That's right, Ms. Ridnouer. I'm talking 'bout you. That was a good class we had today." This student hadn't always been so appreciative of my efforts. Stacey used to arrive late, without supplies but always with plenty of attitude. I admonished her for being late and reminded her about the expected school supplies, but mostly I was working to figure out her passions and her motivators so that I could sprinkle them into her everyday experience in my classroom. When I asked my students to analyze the history of different styles of music, Stacey's group focused on hip-hop. It was this lesson that inspired her to really join our team. Giving her work that she was interested in while maintaining high behavioral expectations helped Stacey reprioritize her academic effort ahead of her negative behavioral choices.

Parents' participation in and out of your classroom wields influence over students because it is their own children and their neighbors' children who are the consumers of your goods and services. While our primary goal is to meet the needs of our students, we must remain mindful of the influence that parents can have on school decisions and encourage parents to use this influence. Parental assertion of power works in concert with school efforts to keep everyone focused on serving all students well.

Gauging Student Attitude and Taking Action

I teach English composition, and when I meet students for the first time, I attempt to gauge their attitude about writing and grammar. In a given classroom, for example, I might find a "This class is an easy *A*" student, an "I love English" student, and a "Whatever my best friend does is good for me, too" student. Each of these students will need a different push from me. Of course, students rarely state their views toward subject matter in quite so explicit a way, and even if they do, they don't provide instructions on the best way to respond to these attitudes.

As I see it, student perceptions as they relate to academic performance can be broken into two categories: (1) students' perception of *whether or not* they understand the material and (2) students' perception of their *ability* to understand the material. Clearly, a student who feels that she doesn't understand something *yet* and a student who feels she's simply incapable of understanding present two different instructional challenges. Once you understand which category a struggling student falls in, you can customize your approach, but your first order of business is to diagnose the source of the disconnect.

▶ Use affective assessment

Ask your students to anonymously respond to a series of questions designed to assess both categories of student perceptions: their understanding of the material and their perception of their ability. Assessment for Learning (AFL), an inventory in three different age categories, ranging from grades 3 to 12, is a quick way to assess how your students approach learning. Find it online at www.ccsso.org.

Rick Stiggins and W. James Popham (2008), the authors of AFL, assert that an inventory like theirs can help a teacher determine both students' academic efficacy and their eagerness to learn. Giving these kinds of assessments before you begin a unit and after you have taught the unit will give you an idea of how your teaching methods are addressing your students' perceptions.

Affective assessment doesn't have to be formal. Your students send messages to you every day about their beliefs in their own abilities, through both their words and their physical movements. Paying attention to what individual students say and do is essential if you hope to respond in ways that effectively address their concerns.

▶ Push students to move from "doing schoolwork" to building knowledge

Many students need to be guided as they develop a love of learning, which can help them cross the bridge from simply doing their schoolwork to acquiring a new and deeper understanding of the material. The grades they receive should become an auxiliary element to their experience, not the main goal. Teach them that your goal is to build their body of knowledge.

Perhaps an affective pre-assessment shows that your students feel overwhelmed when given a large number of instructions at one time. The students don't know how to break a lesson into digestible bits, so they've developed the response of quitting or accepting that they can't understand everything you present to them. In response, you might revise the manner in which you present information within a unit.

Begin by offering an overview of a concept and teaching the details. Summarize, and then let students practice the idea. After a few lessons that follow this model, ratchet up the number of new concepts you are teaching, and ask students to summarize the lesson in their own words. Keep ratcheting up the students' responsibilities in breaking down and summarizing throughout the unit until you reach your students' saturation point. Finally, give students a post-unit affective assessment, and analyze their perception of how they respond to integrating new ideas. Discuss with them how your teaching strategy was in direct response to the results of the affective pre-assessment. They'll feel cared for and heard, and understand the work that goes into the process of constructing knowledge.

▶ Reframe failure as a stepping stone

Students who love the subject you teach are a dream because they are eager to learn more and bring passionate energy to the class. However, problems can arise for this type of student if they fail to meet their own high expectations. Perhaps a student didn't score highly on a test or didn't perform well in a presentation. A student who has always been an academic highflier has a longer way to fall in comparison with one who has a more lukewarm relationship with the subject and a more modest record of success. Give your high-achieving students the opportunity to fail on a small scale in your classroom so that they can bounce back quickly when they fail on a larger scale. They will begin to see failure as a part of the process of understanding. Here are two ways that I build responses to student failure into my practice.

Ideas to Help Students Cope with Failure

• *Plan for drafts in essay assignments.* When my students are assigned an essay, they are required to write three drafts of the essay for a homework grade before I will accept it for an essay grade. This way, if they fail to use proper grammar or develop their thesis statement properly, they have more chances to do the work and receive a good grade.

• *Set up classroom discussions as a "safe space."* When a student shows a lack of understanding about a poem we've read, I can pinpoint the section she needs to reread and ask her to report back to the class the next day. This way, she both comes to understand the material and learns a coping mechanism for handling failure.

▶ Reframe success as a "skipping stone"

Allow proficient students to skip assignments they have clearly mastered. Let the students know that you recognize inherent differences in readiness by giving them some say in assignment choice. If they have received superior grades in one area of the class, then allow them to choose to spend their time focusing on (and coming to excel in) an area in which they are struggling. For example, if a student has received a 95 or above on his math facts drills, exempt him from future drills so that he can spend more time on lessons that break story problems into distinct parts.

▶ Encourage self-direction

Some students, especially in the tween and teenage years, haven't figured out or embraced their own areas of interest. Instead, they find it socially and emotionally safer to simply adopt the same attitudes and interests as their friends. Seek out individuality in all your students. Comment on their personal qualities and make them part of your lesson when possible. For example, I might say, "Your eyes just lit up when we read that poem! I would love to read some of your own words." The idea is to help these students find a personal connection to the content.

Ideas for Encouraging Self-Direction
- Take action on problems before they cause lasting damage.
- Focus on finding a motivator specific to each student.
- Involve parents and students in decision making.
- Follow up and ask students to summarize the lesson learned.

Moving Parents Beyond Traditional Involvement Activities

Chaperoning a field trip, volunteering in the school library, and making cookies for a bake sale are staples of traditional parent involvement, and they are perfectly legitimate and effective means of parental involvement in the school. You can expand traditional parent involvement and transform it into parent engagement, however, by seeking parent leaders who might not appear to fit the template for a standard volunteer parent.

▶ Start small and escalate

Look for those parents who have a passion for making the school environment a place where every student learns. Approach them with an invitation to lead something small, such as helping with a fund-raiser or attending a parent training workshop on upcoming state testing. Some parents will immediately accept your invitations; others will balk. Keep trying. You might hear, "I wasn't born to be a fund-raiser!" Offer the parent the alternative of helping with the organization of the fund-raising operation instead of leading the fund-raiser. You might hear, "I haven't been in school in 15 years, and I like it that way." Highlight the casual nature of the workshop and that there will be no quiz, just information sharing.

▶ Help parents find motivation

One story I like to keep in my back pocket to inspire parents to move beyond what they think they can do in their child's school environment is the story of Dick and Rick Hoyt, told by author Sam Nall (2002). Dick's son, Rick, was born in 1962 with cerebral palsy, and he is a spastic quadriplegic, nonspeaking person. When medical doctors said that young Rick had no intelligence, Dick disagreed and focused on finding a way to connect with his son. Rick displayed a love of sports, so Dick worked to include him in sports even though Dick himself was no athlete. They started with Dick pushing Rick in a five-mile benefit run. They came in next to last. When Dick saw how much Rick enjoyed that experience, he committed himself to regularly including Rick in athletic events. Together, they have competed in marathons, cross-country treks, and triathlons, with Dick pushing Rick in his wheelchair, steering him on their specially made bike, or pulling him on a raft.

Dick didn't lack athletic ability before Rick was born; what he lacked was the motivation. Most likely, your students' parents don't lack the ability to be parent leaders, but they may not see the appeal of the role. As they politely listen to your invitation, they might wonder, "How is this worth my time?" "There has to be someone better qualified than me," or "How is this going to help my child?" Use your interpersonal skills to tap into what motivates each parent, and provide reasons that will help them understand that when positive changes are introduced to a school, they have an impact on every child in that school.

▶ Seek creative solutions built on real motivators

Survey parents to gain an understanding of what issue or issues might be dissuading them from greater degrees of engagement. Your school's leadership team can create a survey for each family and make it available on the school's website or in the form of a paper sent home with the eldest child from each family. Seek answers to questions such as these:

- Are you currently involved in volunteer activities that occur during school hours?
  - If not, what would encourage you to do so?
  - What kind of volunteer information would you find helpful?
  - What hours would you be available to volunteer?
  - What types of activities would you prefer to participate in?

By taking the time to ask these questions and responding in ways that address parental concerns, you will invite every parent voice to contribute to the "school chorus," creating music that truly reflects your school community.

Maximizing Your Increased-Engagement Reach

Each student needs your individual attention, but practically speaking, no one has the time or the energy to individualize every assignment and find a personal connection between every child and every lesson. However, you do have time to be intentional about being aware of those students who need more challenge or individualization by prioritizing the different needs of your students. It's understandable that you might fall into a pattern of giving all your attention to the boisterous students, the low-achieving students, and the gifted students, but you have to push yourself to keep each student on your radar so that they each get an opportunity to become their best self in your classroom. Look for ways to solve problems that affect many of your students, and then you will have the time to differentiate your lessons for those students with specialized needs.

Improving Everybody's Rate of Retention

Your instruction casts a wider net if you work to improve each student's rate of retention. Do this by infusing meaning into academic experiences. Giving each student the opportunity to showcase his or her understanding of the subject in a safe environment is one way to do this. It helps students use the intelligence they were born with and become comfortable working in different contexts.

David Sousa (2005) found that how information is managed affects the learner's retention rate. He noted that students' average information retention rate after a 24-hour period depends greatly on how the information has been presented:

Lecture:	5%
Reading:	10%
Audiovisual:	20%
Demonstration:	30%
Discussion group:	50%
Practice by doing:	75%
Teaching others—immediate use of learning:	90% (p. 95)

When you create your lesson plans, keep these retention rates in mind. I'm not saying that lecture is out of the question, but be mindful that when you choose to present information to your students in this way, you will need to follow up with a method of presentation that has a higher retention rate, such as a discussion group or practice by doing.

▶ Personalize material for students

When a student is struggling with a new concept, look for clues to discover the source of the problem and offer a solution that incorporates the student's interests. A former student of mine, Ben, started the semester full of self-doubt and concern about grasping the finer details in class. Ben was a quiet but very willing student. After working with him, I realized that he digested new information best with short explanations that related to a topic he was interested in. He had written about his interest in photography, so when I was explaining how to gauge whether his writing was too specific or too general, I used the metaphor of a camera lens to explain how to focus on main points when writing an essay. I encouraged him to focus his lens for readers, so they can understand what he means. He understood my words immediately, and his writing became more complex and interesting, reflecting who he was. Listen for your students' interests, and weave those interests into your instruction.

▶ Stretch everyone

Traditionally, the gifted students have been the students invited to mentally stretch themselves, participating in high-interest projects while the rest of the student body churns through the traditional curriculum. Schools in Syosset, New York, are approaching enrichment another way. They offer clusters of enrichment to all of their students. The program is modeled after the schoolwide enrichment approach designed by Joseph Renzulli (Renzulli & Reis, 2007). He is the director of the National Research Center on the Gifted and Talented, which works to design "high-end learning" experiences for all students.

Renzulli believes that students need a variety of opportunities to be successful in school. With the increasing emphasis on basic skills and testing, students need outlets for learning in a variety of ways that engage them in rigorous content. He has found that this type of enrichment gives students the opportunity to foster talents important to their development, such as creative thinking, critical thinking, and problem solving. Each of these talents promotes students' learning of traditional subject matter. When a student performs a song about Christopher Columbus instead of writing a traditional book report, she learns the material with the added bonus of thinking creatively. When another student plays a table drum wearing the costume of his native India, he encourages critical thinking in himself and his listeners when he answers questions about how to play the drum and why people in his culture dress in light colors.

Enrichment for everyone gives students pleasurable associations with school, relaxing the students and opening them up to the learning process. When a student is filtering each lesson through an "I'm bored"—or worse, "I'm stupid"—mantra, it is very difficult for learning to take place. Tapping into student passions silences the negative mantra. Encouraging students to incorporate ideas learned outside the classroom while they are in the classroom pushes students to trust their abilities. They develop hidden parts of themselves by completing addition problems and sentence completion exercises on their own.

Looking for New Leaders

Cliques don't end with high school graduation. Elementary, middle, and high schools alike will find that there are groups of parents who are natural leaders and happily accept volunteer opportunities. It is the school's responsibility to offer volunteer opportunities to parents from a variety of racial, demographic, economic, and religious backgrounds. It's essential for students and parents to see volunteers who look like them, for this reinforces their sense of belonging. In addition, parents need to see that the school doesn't favor the efforts of one kind of parent over others. When all parents feel more comfortable in schools, we should see a change in the sad situation reported in a 2005 National PTA public service announcement:

"While many parents support learning at home, only one in four parents is actively involved in their children's schools. That number shrinks to one in nine among working parents whose schedules often present additional challenges."

▶ Acknowledge parents' role as educational partners

Karen Mapp (2002) offers insight into how you can engage parents as leaders. In her research, she found that when teachers engage in caring and trusting relationships with parents in a manner that recognizes parents as partners in the educational development of children, these relationships enhance parents' desire to be involved and influence how they participate in their children's educational development. Through a process of welcoming parents into the school, honoring their participation, and connecting with them through a focus on the children and their learning, teachers can nurture a parent's willingness to engage.

A good place to start is to ask parent leaders to focus on the four factors Reginald Clark (1993) has identified as accounting for nearly half of the variation between low-achieving and high-achieving students:

1. Parent knowledge about homework assignments
2. Parent perception of child's engagement in homework
3. Child knowledge of how to use a dictionary
4. Parent expectations for child's education

Ideas for How Parents Can Address Clark's Four Factors

• *Lobby your parent-teacher organization to buy homework journals for every student.* Parents would be asked to sign and date this journal every night, and teachers would be encouraged to set up a system of rewards and consequences based on student use of the journal.

• *Encourage teacher-parent dialogue about homework.* A parent leadership committee could generate a list of discussion starters that teachers might occasionally include in homework journals for parents to respond to when they sign the journal. Parents can be asked to comment on different elements of their child's work, including neatness, organization, length, and difficulty. Teachers can offer their insight into how the student homework reflects the student's true ability. Here is a sample list of questions teachers can include in homework journals:

* Circle one of the following choices to describe your child's response to his homework assignment. Add comments if you'd like: *Easy   Hard   Just Right*
* How can I help your child learn best?
* Are you happy with the neatness and organization of your child's homework?
* What resources can I offer you to help homework time go more smoothly?

In addition, parent leaders could provide questions that they themselves have thought of during homework time. Their input is vital to this exercise because their questions are more likely to reflect the concerns of other parents in the community than questions generated by a teacher.

• *Inquire explicitly into how concrete skills are being taught.* The skills Clark highlights include using a dictionary, writing an outline, memorizing multiplication tables, reading a clock and a thermometer, and using an online search engine. If parent-teacher discussion reveals that students are struggling in a particular area, the parent leadership team can then develop a response, such as assignments that require practice with the skill, workshops for parents and their children to demonstrate the importance of the skill, or opportunities to use the school computer lab for additional practice.

• *Ask the school to explicitly communicate to parents that high parent expectations lead to higher achievement.* Parents need to see this message repeatedly, spoken by teachers, published on the school website, and included in newsletters. Creating events that promote the belief that their school is a special place, along with ceremonies to recognize high achievers, will provide motivation for the entire school community.

How to Use Negative Attitudes as a Catalyst for Productive Change

When you approach a roadblock while driving, there is usually a sign telling you that you will have to slow down ahead. Unfortunately, roadblocks to engagement are not so clearly labeled, and the reasons behind them are sometimes difficult to figure out. In my experience, the clues to why a student or parent resists engagement will add up quickly enough if you just look for them patiently. They can be heard, seen, read, or even sensed: a word, blinking eyes, disparaging language, or feelings of tension. By slowing down and acknowledging the signs that your senses pick up, you will help students and parents change negative beliefs into positive action.

Just as you seek resources to support student learning, search out those resources that will spread the message that parent input can help students. The beginning of the school year is the logical starting point for cultivating parent leaders from your pool of parents. As you develop relationships with parents, you will be able to identify individual parents who have leadership skills that could benefit the school. Remain mindful that parents can influence school decisions, and encourage the responsible use of this power.

Figuring Out—and Changing—Students' "Truth"

What students believe is true about themselves can serve to either limit or expand their potential for success in the classroom. Unfortunately, students don't wear t-shirts that broadcast their limiting beliefs in bold letters. We have to ask questions that challenge the identity they present in the class and listen to the connotations of the words they choose. Take the "Nobody from my family has graduated from high school" or "Math isn't for me" statements as expressions of fear—which students need your help to overcome. Before they can fully digest your lessons, students have to be freed from the limiting beliefs that prevent them from learning effectively. Become aware of these beliefs and challenge them so that your students can begin to entertain the possibility of being successful in your classroom—and in any classroom.

▶ Look for the source of limiting beliefs

Do they stem from an academic concern? Issues of gender or race? Religion? Friends? Family? Economics? Limiting beliefs can involve academic as well as nonacademic areas of your students' lives. Become aware of the particular beliefs that your students might hold as a group, and also take the time to name them when students use them to make decisions in their lives. By addressing these issues in your classroom, you will be taking steps to free your students' capable selves from their own self-imposed restrictions.

▶ Address academic limiting beliefs by challenging them directly

Failure in a subject, especially at an early age, can convince a student that the particular subject is not his or her "thing." Students can convince themselves that it is OK to fail in one subject with the platitude, "We can't be good at everything." When you hear students say words like these, have a response at the ready that will push them to reevaluate the validity of the platitude and how it is keeping them from being less than the best version of themselves. A few that I use regularly are "You're only as good as you think you are" (The Whispers); "Change your thoughts, change your life" (Wayne Dyer); and "Mistakes are the portals of discovery" (James Joyce).

Small improvements can appreciate in value over time. It would be nice if we didn't have to repeat, remind, and attend to students. It would be grand if students would learn a lesson the first time we taught it. But learning doesn't occur that way. It happens in fits and starts, or it inches along. Continuing to push students to accept how they can learn new ideas will help them optimize their learning potential. John Wooden, the legendary UCLA basketball coach, offered this description of learning: "When you improve a little each day, eventually big things occur.... Not tomorrow, not the next day, but eventually a big gain is made. Don't look for the big, quick improvement. Seek the small improvement one day at a time. That's the only way it happens—and when it happens, it lasts" (Nater & Gallimore, 2005, p. 52).

▶ Discuss nonacademic limiting beliefs as a whole class

Often, students internalize limiting beliefs about school achievement based on cultural, gender, religious, or economic identifiers. In these cases, I suggest addressing the issue indirectly within the context of the curriculum

Here's an example. My student Sheena is black and a teenage single mother. She didn't believe me when I told her that she could become anything she wanted to. One day, when the students and I were discussing the difference between transcendentalism and determinism, I asked the students who they thought held political clout in our country. They agreed that white men were typically the ones in power. I pushed the discussion to focus on race for Sheena's benefit by asking, "If most politicians are white, how did we end up with a black president?" After a pause, one student suggested that Barack Obama didn't let the past determine his future; he was a transcendentalist. I tried to gauge how Sheena was feeling about the discussion, but she sat there with a poker face. She didn't comment then, but during a break two weeks later, her darting eyes caught mine, and she said, "Ms. Ridnouer, I am not saying this to suck up, but..." She paused. "I admire you."

I started to respond with a thank-you, but she interrupted me.

"I mean, I never thought I would respect a white person," she said. "But after your talk about people in power, I respect you."

I thanked Sheena and said I hoped she would continue to consider my words in class. The other students started filing back in, and the moment was over. But its effect was far from over. My sense is that it led Sheena to begin thinking about the way she perceived other aspects of her life. She went on to pass my class with an A— not too shabby, especially considering it was the first course she'd taken since the birth of her baby. Who knows where Sheena will land?

Harnessing Parent Influence

Instead of ignoring parents when you overhear them ranting in the school parking lot and sighing as you walk swiftly to your classroom, take heed of what these parents are saying and offer them an outlet for their concerns. The parent-teacher organization, school leadership teams, and school improvement teams can be a place where complaints are addressed as parents learn more about practices and policies that frustrate them.

▶ Support good practice

Encourage your principal to create mechanisms to support individual parents' efforts to become more effective members of the community by offering skill-building opportunities. This could include giving parents the opportunity to practice making a presentation to the school board about an item up for a vote, such as changing the school districts, amending the busing policy, or implementing a districtwide reading program. Creating a base of parent leaders who are strong public speakers gives your school sincere advocates whose opinion will make a difference.

▶ Be a link in the chain of command

You know the chain of command within your school district, but don't assume that your parents do. I have worked with many parents who believe that if the teacher and the principal cannot solve a problem, then the next step involves calling the superintendent. Share the chain of command in your school with parent leaders, and they can then share this information with families in the school community. Ensuring that this information is on the FAQ page of the school's website will also help parents address problems in a more direct fashion.

▶ Advertise opportunities to be the school's voice

Encourage parents to write about their opinion on school matters in letters to the editor and other media sources such as community newspapers, neighborhood newsletters, or even your school's own newspaper. A confident, passionate parent responding to a journalist's question about why school funding should not be cut is an effective means of providing the parent perspective on the real consequences of cutting or reducing school resources. To a policymaker, increasing class size from 25 to 30 might not seem that big of a difference initially, but that policymaker will understand how big a difference it is when a parent points out that his exceptional child will not get the individualized instruction she needs with five additional students in the class.

▶ Work with the leadership teams

Many schools have leadership teams that include parents, teachers, and at least one administrator. These teams are designed to bring together interested parties within a school community. Done the right way, parents are given a chance to dream a little bit about what they would like to see at their child's school while teachers and the administrator focus on how to get a problem solved. The synergy of the two can create solutions that are perfectly fitted for that school environment. Encouraging creative thought processes during meetings helps parents and teachers both find solutions that suit the sensibilities of the school's families.

While leadership teams focus on an array of issues, subgroups of the leadership team can focus their attention on specific initiatives such as the following:

- Evaluating current fund-raisers
- Finding solutions to challenges created by funding changes
- Prioritizing teacher wish lists
- Reviewing and making recommendations for new curricula, including audiovisual and written materials, and new educational software to be used by students
- Updating school policy
- Ensuring that exceptional students are regularly receiving necessary services

Inviting subgroups of leadership teams to attend teacher training workshops with you and your colleagues is another way to strengthen the school community and give everyone a common base of knowledge, along with the tools to put that knowledge to work. To begin, focus on inviting parent leaders to workshops that explore parent involvement topics such as the following:

- What is a parent leader? What are the parent leader's roles and responsibilities?
- Establishing and building partnerships
- Creating effective teams through conflict resolution and shared responsibility
- Defining shared leadership between teacher and parent

▶ Make parent leadership an event

National Parent Leadership Month takes place each February, giving you a midyear opportunity to conduct a large-scale invitation for parent leaders who have emerged during the first part of the school year. Another event idea is to nominate current parent leaders for recognition. Include a review of the nominated parents' accomplishments in the school newspaper, and encourage a joint parent-student vote on the topic. This will create a buzz around the event and boost the number of attendees. In addition to rewarding a worthy volunteer, the recognition will inspire other parents to get involved, thereby creating a forum to discuss more opportunities for parent leadership.

▶ Form parent focus groups

Each school year brings new issues to a school community. One year, the school might be working through a renovation. The next, the school might be working to improve test scores in math. Support the idea of forming parent focus groups to address specific issues as they arise. Your school will benefit from the parents' inherent child-centered focus and their fresh perspective on the issue. Parents also might have skill sets that are different from those of school personnel, since parents come from a variety of professional backgrounds. This diversity can prove helpful in finding creative solutions to common problems. Parent focus groups can be formed to address issues such as raising test scores, school safety, homework policies, gang prevention, and outreach to homeless, impoverished, or unemployed families in the school community.

Cultivating Leadership Boosts Your Own Effectiveness

It can be intimidating to invite students and parents to become leaders within the classroom and the school community. You are the one with the training; you are the one "in charge" of your students. But remember why you became a teacher. Most likely it wasn't because you wanted to make every school decision yourself. Instead, you probably became a teacher because in your unique way you wanted to inspire your students to become lifelong learners. Inviting parents to be decision makers in partnership with you and your colleagues gives you the insight, the assistance, and the time to do what you are meant to do—inspire your students.

Although most of the suggestions in this chapter are unrelated to curriculum, they are all a means to cover the curriculum. Unless teachers address students' limiting beliefs, and unless parents feel a sense of support for the school, the richest curriculum becomes a wasted opportunity. Change students' and parents' perspectives on how much they can change their current level of engagement, and you will see academic achievement rise.

Extensions

Successful teachers are always on the lookout for clues that will help guide students toward even greater success. They cultivate compassionate, personalized responses that show students and parents what they can gain from being members of the classroom community, and they look beyond the school walls to see where else positive support and services might be found. In Chapter 9, we look at ways to model, illustrate, and extend the benefits of learning community by opening the doors to the resources and support of the wider world.

Tapping Outside Resources

All our progress is an unfolding, like a vegetable bud.
You have first an instinct, then an opinion, then a knowledge
as the plant has root, bud, and fruit. Trust the instinct to the end,
though you can render no reason.

✳ RALPH WALDO EMERSON ✳

Macroteaching is a term that describes what a teacher does when he or she pulls resources from the larger community—its institutions and religious and civic organizations—to help bring out students' strengths and connect them to larger, bigger academic ideas.

When students see their parents and fellow community members participating in activities such as Junior Achievement or a lunch buddy program, they see school as a worthwhile place to be. Adults benefit from seeing how their efforts can directly affect the students' lives; this positive effect in turn encourages them to become further involved. With prompting from you, parents might begin to see how their connections with the larger community can benefit the school, thus providing opportunities for macroteaching that has concrete benefits for your students, such as event sponsorship or internship opportunities. Give your students the gift of macroteaching and you give them the gift of connecting their lives to the larger world—a world that has a place for them.

In this chapter, we'll look at strategies for macroteaching and working with the larger community to meet the needs of your school and each of its students. The key questions are as follows:

1. How do I share the responsibility of teaching with outsiders?

2. How do I maintain my role as teacher when I share responsibility with students and their parents?

How to Share the Responsibility of Teaching

Think of the wide variety of interests and needs that your students have, and then seek out community members who might make contributions in these areas. You might feel overwhelmed at first. Stay true to the philosophy that community members can enrich your students' education with specialized support. And remind yourself of your intent: to help your students become their best selves and realize their potential in the world.

Considering Your Resources

Your school guidance counselor or school psychologist can be a good starting place for names of people who can work with you, but don't be afraid to dream big when you are brainstorming whom you would like to see interacting with your students. Here are some questions to ask yourself:

• *Who can connect the dots?* Which individuals or organizations in your community can highlight practical applications of academic content and help students see the value in "boring" subjects?

• *Who can inspire my students?* Which individuals or organizations can connect with your students' passions and provide motivation in a different way than you do?

- *Who can give my students the tools that I am not equipped to give?* Who in your community has specialized training that will specifically address roadblocks to individual students' academic success?

▶ **Seek out professional practitioners in curricular areas**

Poll your parents about their professional and volunteer experiences to create a database to track resources for different curricular topics. Parents, or people parents know, might be willing to lead a seminar about the practical application of class lessons. This type of community involvement shows students that you want to help them make sense of the world around them.

Parents might be connected to people who work in specialized fields or participate in specialized crafts. Each of these parent connections are potential sources of enrichment for your students. Create a list of community members and ask parents to identify individuals who might be willing to take on specific tasks or crafts. When you need a professional related to one of these, contact the parent who circled that task and ask him or her to reach out to that community member personally.

Here are some examples of community members who could make a difference in and out of your classroom.

Elementary School

- An avid gardener could talk about the joy of eating food grown by your own hands during the time you teach a unit on the food pyramid.
- A local athlete could run with and motivate the students when they are preparing for the annual Presidential Physical Fitness Test.

Middle School

- An artist could share the process involved in throwing a pot during a unit on measuring circumference.

• A local writer could talk to students about how she finds her subjects and her supporting details during the introduction of a lesson on effective paragraph writing.

High School

• An accountant could teach a practical lesson on income tax during your unit on the American Revolution and the Boston Tea Party.

• A paralegal could be asked to allow a few of your astute researchers to shadow him or her for the day.

▶ Seek professional practitioners in noncurricular areas

Find community members who have the professional or life experience that will inspire students to be their best selves. These people might be underdogs who have come out on top, professional athletes who value education, or hard workers who have put in time and effort to bring about their success. If the parents themselves don't fit into such categories, look for parents with auxiliary connections to highly successful people. A friend of mine works in athletic orthotics and knows many of the professional football players in my area. Many times, he has arranged for these athletes to come in and give a motivational talk to my students about why they need to work hard in school. However I choose to teach my students about what it takes to be successful, the message is amplified when it is reinforced by someone who stands 6 feet, 5 inches tall.

▶ Present tutoring as an investment that pays dividends

Some students have needs that you can't fully remediate in the classroom, even with the clarification of an IEP or a 504 Plan. Tutors, counselors, and educational therapists are great resources when students need help in a particular area. Being prepared with the name of a professional who can help a student outside the classroom shows parents that you, too, are a professional and that you only want the best for their child. Here, a guidance counselor or school psychologist will be a valuable resource. In addition, keep your ears open as your students' parents share information about professionals they have worked with. Add these professionals to your list, along with names that colleagues might suggest at a staff meeting or ones that neighbors might mention at a barbeque.

When parents express concern about whether or not their child needs outside services, be sure to have evidence on hand to support your suggestion. For example, the student who is having difficulty with written expression will have ample evidence in his writing folder. Showing parents their child's work next to the work of an average student in your class will help them see the disparities clearly. If the parents don't think the services are necessary, suggest the perspective that tutoring now is an investment in their child that will pay off in dividends of decreased frustration and increased motivation. These are incalculable but palpable rewards for any student.

Cultivating Parent-Driven Partnerships Within the Larger Community

Charitable organizations, businesses, hospitals, and churches provide services to schools in many communities. You might read about events in the newspaper or hear about them on the news and wonder, "How do I get that going in my own school?" Follow up on that question by drafting parents to help tap the resources of the community organizations that they support.

▶ Identify community resources that meet specific needs

Tapping into community resources requires time, effort, persistence, and organization, but the rewards are many. Encourage your school to use parent leaders to involve members of the larger community. These parents will serve as excellent spokespersons as they advocate for the school to community groups, churches, and civic clubs, and communicate what's happening in the building. They are credible voices to others in the community. In addition, as members of the community, they have an "in" that you might not have.

Encourage parents to use their business connections and skills to support the school by inviting business partners to student art shows, holiday programs, and dramatic performances. To go further, hold these programs in community facilities such as churches and community centers to bring the entire community together. This will encourage the most important kind of support that a school could ask for—a compassionate response to students. This compassion will encourage businesses and other community members to donate money, resources, and volunteer hours. This kind of support can bring about a positive change in student achievement in any school, especially when the support is focused on a specific concern.

Start with those organizations that your students' parents are already involved in. Their church or community center might already have a list of volunteers who are willing to contribute volunteer hours in the community. Churches might be able to share space for school events in their building; your local parks and recreation group could conduct fitness workshops for students after school or during school holidays. The local hospital could be invited to parent-teacher organization meetings to conduct a series of workshops on health-related issues relevant to the needs of your school's families. Allow yourself to dream a little bit about what your students need, and then think about who would be able to meet that need. You will never know whom you can recruit if you don't ask.

Schools can ask businesspeople to share their specialized skills in shared programming, such as a school-to-work program, a mentoring program, or service learning opportunities. In addition, schools can ask businesspeople to use their worksite to display and distribute information about schools and parent involvement. Ask permission to exhibit student artwork or student projects in businesses' storefront windows.

Another option is to ask local civic groups to provide dynamic speakers to talk to students about the realities of the workplace, including information about what they look for in interviews, their forecast of future job opportunities, and what education they require from their employees. After a presentation from a member of the business community, ask students to write thank-you notes or, even better, to collaborate on a letter to the editor of the local paper about the generous business partner. The latter provides good publicity to the business (always an excellent way to show gratitude) and may spur involvement from other community members.

▶ Spread out the resources within a community

In Charlotte, North Carolina, a unique partnership has been formed between two schools—Elizabeth Lane Elementary and Thomasboro Elementary. Since 1998, Elizabeth Lane Elementary's parent volunteers have traveled nearly 20 miles from their neighborhood to provide needed items and emotional support to students, parents, and staff at Thomasboro Elementary. The differences between the two schools are dramatic: Thomasboro has 384 students, 94 percent of whom qualify for free or reduced-price lunch. Elizabeth Lane has 984 students, 6 percent of whom qualify for free or reduced-price lunch.

The partnership, which began as a "lunch buddy" program, has become a relationship that attends to the students', teachers', and parents' needs on many levels. Elizabeth Lane has held coat drives where more than 350 coats have been donated. Its book drive netted thousands of books for Thomasboro's library and the school's accelerated reader program. Elizabeth Lane parent volunteers facilitate the relationship between Thomasboro and community business partners, who have funded fun fairs and t-shirt rewards, helping to build school spirit and inspire a deep connection between students and their academic life.

Any community that has disparate economic neighborhoods can create this kind of partnership. The students receive the support they need to be successful, and the parents benefit from watching their efforts bring about true growth in both children and the community. The more tightly connected students feel to their community, the more likely they are to become productive members of that community and advocate for its well-being as adults.

▶ Seek different perspectives

Extra sets of eyes brings the school's vision full circle. One of the benefits of involving parents in the school is the added vision that parents contribute to planning school events. It is easy for us professionals to get mired in the daily business of ticking activities off our teaching to-do list instead of intentionally giving each activity the time and care it deserves. Another set of eyes can provide focus.

At my sons' school, the parent-teacher organization works hard to supplement both the academic and nonacademic lessons that the teachers provide each day. At one meeting, a parent raised the point that the events we'd sponsored so far—fun, community-building events and bake sales to raise activity funds—benefitted students but didn't given them the opportunity to give back to the larger community.

We decided to hold an event that encouraged students to expend energy for the benefit of a nonprofit charitable organization focused on building educational infrastructure all over the world. The subsequent historical scavenger hunt in a community park, sponsored by individuals and local businesses, raised money and goodwill, and taught our students about the importance of service work. It was a parent's suggestion that made this possible. The students learned an immensely valuable lesson—one that might have been neglected had the parents not brought to our attention the need to teach students the importance of service work.

How to Maintain Authority When Sharing Responsibility

Sharing the classroom with students, their parents, and community members can feel overwhelming. You might wonder, "What if I spend all this time gathering personal information on my students and they still fail? What if parents working with their children at home 'undo' some of what I'm trying to achieve? What if students misbehave and precious instruction time is wasted?"

These are all legitimate concerns, but first let's look more deeply into the benefits of macroteaching. In addition to interpersonal and

academic benefits for students, macroteaching can further parental and community support of the school and of you. The synergy
between what matters to your students and what matters to the
adults in their lives will give heightened meaning to the ideas you
hold students responsible for in the classroom. Involving people
with expertise in a subject you are teaching gives veracity to your
words and makes a much stronger impression on students' understanding than simply teaching it on your own.

Making Macroteaching Meaningful to Students

Engaging the larger community can be beneficial to both the school
and the business or nonprofit that you invite to participate. While
your partners have the resources to donate materials and expertise
to promote academic pursuits at the school, your students are a
source of people power that can be harnessed to support the goals of
the larger community. This is a mutualism in its best form—where
both parties can survive well enough without one another, but with
one another, they can reach their full potential.

▶ Do "undercover work" that works

When you observe your students and collect information, you
do it for one purpose: to determine how you can best meet your
their needs. Don't worry about how much time it takes you to collect this information; noticing one detail can make the difference in
whether a student chooses to learn from you or not. You will actually save time in the end because the student will be working with
you instead of having to be convinced every time that he or she is
worthwhile in your eyes.

▶ Steer students toward a problem they can solve

Finding our place in this world is what growing up is all about.
This place can be beneficial or detrimental to a student, depending
on the influences in the student's life. Why not be proactive and

offer positive ways for students to find their place by offering positive outlets for their time and energy? Find outlets that encourage student participation and engage their skill sets so they can see how their actions can have an impact on the larger community.

When students feel that their efforts can change the outcome of a situation, they are more likely to participate. I offer my students ideas on improving the larger community throughout the semester. Recently, half of our community's libraries were slated to be closed. I shared my despair over this and the steps I was taking to help reverse this decision. I invited them to join me in voicing concern to the public officials involved in this decision. The students have encouraged their friends and family members to write their county commissioners, and they participated in protest in front of the recently opened library that will be closed soon if money isn't raised and the decision reversed.

Students want to be with passionate people who want to initiate change. Be one of those people, steer your students toward opportunities for them to be with others, and watch them become passionate themselves.

Clarifying Roles for Yourself and for Parents

The right relationship between parents and school personnel involves parents remaining parents, and school personnel remaining educators. No one is asking parents to "do the teacher's job" or teachers to be parental substitutes. By advocating for parents to regularly connect home and school, you help send the message that learning is everybody's number-one priority. Setting this connection as a given principle makes the invitation of engagement difficult to ignore.

▶ Be specific about the needs you will fulfill

Telling your students' parents that you are there to help them is a nice idea, but not very effective at increasing parent participation. Find out what parents need from you to become more engaged at school. Look for clues and ask directly. Then figure out where you can realistically make a difference.

▶ Lobby for a facultywide support policy

Any interaction time with a parent can potentially influence that parent's decision to become engaged in his or her child's education. Keep this in mind even when you interact with parents whose child you do not teach. You could be that one teacher who showed those parents that they were needed.

I encourage you to lobby your principal to intentionally foster a sense of community in your school by promoting the idea that every teacher is there to support every student in the school, not just the students they are assigned to teach. The leadership team could be given the task of creating a slogan that promotes this campaign to parents, encouraging them to ask any teacher, administrator, or school employee for assistance. "Every teacher supports EVERY family" would be a great place to start.

▶ Provide resources and referrals, as appropriate

Sometimes parents need resources outside the school realm. We've talked a lot in this book about the tremendous difference a teacher can make, but there are some challenges that will be beyond you—points at which the way to make a difference is to steer parents toward those who can provide the help they really need.

If there is an overriding concern for many of the families in your classroom, consider asking your principal to design parent support groups with volunteer coordinators who are trained to lead compassionate responses to parent concerns. With the recent rise in unemployment, bankruptcy, and foreclosure, stress could be high in your students' homes. Students feel this stress and need tools to cope effectively.

Talk to your school's guidance counselor about parent support services within the community or ones that could be made available at the school. You can also talk to your school leadership team to hire facilitators from outside the school to work on campus to give parents the comfort of addressing a concern within the surroundings of their child's school. Providing this resource will strengthen parents' trust in you and give them what they need to enrich their family's lives.

Continuing to Learn

Occasionally putting ourselves in our students' shoes is a good way to see the many different areas of one's life that macroteaching can affect. In 1991, I was codirector of a camp for Native American children ages 13 to 18 who had been exposed to drug or alcohol abuse. The camp was located in the Black Hills of South Dakota, and it was surrounded by a lush forest full of wildlife. It stood in stark contrast to the desolate landscape of the reservation where the students lived.

I wrote and taught the curriculum with a drug and alcohol counselor and served as a camp counselor at the same time. Mrs. D'Angelo, the drug and alcohol counselor there, is a former addict and one of the most compassionate people I have ever met. Before we greeted the kids, she told me, "They look normal, but rest assured, these kids need us. This week will change their lives."

I looked at these beautiful kids and wondered about the accuracy of Mrs. D'Angelo's words. The kids were all smiles and shiny eyes. A handsome boy bounced a basketball, and five others soon joined in. The girls twittered around like nervous sandpipers on the beach, beautiful but not wanting to be singled out for attention.

They looked like normal kids. I wondered how they could possibly have come from homes where they had suffered physical and emotional abuse, but their responses to our survey indicated that every one of these kids had a family member who was an alcoholic or a drug addict. Many of them had been neglected or abused. We dove into planning mode to create a week chockfull of lessons that would inspire these students to make healthy choices when they returned home.

During that week, we discussed drugs and addiction, we hiked the Black Hills, we swam in a nearby pool, and best of all, we created a community. Since I was a counselor in addition to my codirector job, I was with the kids all day and all night. I had the chance to get to know them as we talked long past the time for lights out. They told me whom they had crushes on, we teased one girl for her blue silk sheets, and we all wished out loud for some change in our lives. We had a dance at the end of the week, and when Jonathan, a shy 10-year-old, asked me to teach him a few dance moves, I felt as though I had arrived as a teacher.

By the end of the week, I was emotionally spent. I felt privileged to have worked with these children, and I hoped that something they heard that week would help them make their lives better. Father Mike, an Episcopal priest who led daily services at the camp, talked to me about my hope for my students. "Katy, they might look like they don't hear you, but it's sinking in," he assured me. "One day they'll hear your words. It could be in a month; it could be in five years."

As I hugged the campers goodbye, I assured them each that they were loved. They each hugged back, signaling that they had indeed heard me. They knew that their home circumstances did not have to dictate their future. I wondered if this knowledge would be enough. I prayed that they would use the knowledge as a tool to dig themselves out of a bad situation, to build better lives for themselves, and to be shining stars in their community.

Recalling this lesson when I am in the classroom reminds me to be mindful of what circumstances can't dictate: the gifts that students are born with. A natural ability to build or a gift with numbers can be nurtured no matter what type of home life a student has. Their backgrounds might be different from my own, but when their eyes light up in understanding, our differences don't matter. Only the learning matters.

The leap from impossible to possible is smaller than most students believe. They don't know what they don't know. They don't know that they are unaware of programs in the community designed to keep them safe, to keep them engaged, to keep them kids. They don't know that childhood is not supposed to be anything more than what they are experiencing in this moment. Ignorance is part of the beauty and the tragedy of childhood, because it keeps children from knowing the dangerous parts of life, but also keeps out the light when they are covered in darkness. Shed some light on your students by making them aware of what your community has to offer them if only they would ask.

Conclusion

Be the Difference, Be the Advocate

Be the change you want to see in the world.

✳ MAHATMA GANDHI ✳

Throughout history we have seen that with concentrated effort, a small number of people can create meaningful change. A striking example is the group of 12 men who formed an antislavery movement in England in May 1787. The odds were against them, but they were committed to their cause. They used a variety of strategies to send their message. They wrote petitions, conducted leaflet campaigns, spoke out publicly, sold antislavery merchandise, and boycotted goods produced by slaves. In the end, the abolitionist movement grew and led to the end of slavery in the 19th century.

Margaret Mead encapsulates this principle with the words, "Never doubt that a small group of thoughtful, committed citizens can change the world. Indeed, it's the only thing that ever has." Every day a teacher says, "Good morning, class," that teacher has the opportunity to change the world for those students; extending the same greeting to parents can change the world for the teacher, the student, the parents, the school, and even the entire community.

How powerfully our education system would change if every teacher were to become an everyday advocate of learning—if every teacher would look for unique ways to engage students and parents in learning, and to connect them to the school community and to a successful school experience. Let's revolutionize education by bringing every student and every parent into the education fold. Issue yourself a personal challenge: "If engagement advocacy is to be, it is up to me." I wish the best for you, your students, and your students' parents.

Acknowledgments

In my roles as teacher and parent, I have come into contact with so many caring, insightful, and motivating people who have inspired me to write this book.

Thank you to all the teachers, students, and parents whose success stories helped to shape my understanding of the many perspectives that parent engagement entails. Many of their contributions reached me in response to Eric Frazier's "On Family" column published in the August 30, 2005, edition of *The Charlotte Observer,* in which he wrote about my book idea and encouraged his readers to share their stories with me. Thank you, Mr. Frazier. Other stories came from colleagues, friends, and family. Whichever way your story presented itself to me, I thank you for it.

I am deeply indebted to the members of the Parent Leadership Network in Charlotte, North Carolina, who so eloquently professed their passion for parent involvement during my intensive training with their group. While in operation, the Charlotte Parent Leadership Network worked to show parent leaders how to help create and sustain the schoolhouse conditions necessary for every student to reach and exceed academic expectation. Each of the ladies who trained me—Margaret Carnes, Carolyn Allred, Cheryl Pulliam, and Michelle Belt—embodies the spirit of how caring for children, *everyone's children,* can create quality education for all.

I am so grateful for the parent involvement experiences in my own children's schools. At Elizabeth Lane Elementary in Matthews, North Carolina, I was first initiated in how to become a successful partner with my child's school. At Oakhurst Elementary in Charlotte, I was embraced as a partner in creating curricula and implementing ideas on the leadership team. At Aravon School in County Wicklow, Ireland, my ideas for fund-raising and student workshops were welcomed and applauded. And at Providence Spring Elementary and Crestdale Middle, two of North Carolina's premier schools, I have been afforded many volunteer opportunities to try out strategies and generate new ones. Thank you to each of these schools for welcoming me as a contributing member of your learning community.

The education researchers Joyce Epstein, Jane Henderson, Sandra Christenson, Susan Sheridan, Janine Bempechat, and Bernard Weiner are but a few of the people to whom I owe a debt of gratitude. Each reinforced my intuition that engaging parents in their children's education would benefit not only their own children but also every student attending that school.

Thank you to ASCD for enthusiastically embracing the publication of this book. Special thanks to Scott Willis and Carolyn Pool. My unending thanks and praise goes to Katie Martin, my editor with the all-seeing eye, who pushes me to express what I mean to express when I haven't yet fully expressed it.

And finally, thank you to my dear family members, who have all supported my efforts to write about, research, and experience this topic. Without my husband's generous understanding, my children's constant cheerleading, and my parents' unending enthusiasm, this book would not have been possible.

My aim is to encourage teachers to reassess how they engage students and parents in and out of the classroom. Each of the aforementioned organizations and people has helped me to stretch my boundaries as both a parent and a teacher. It is my hope that teachers are inspired to do the same.

References

Askildson, L. (2005). Effects of humor in the language classroom: Humor as a pedagogical tool in theory and practice. *The Arizona Working Papers in Secondary Language Acquisition & Teaching, 12,* 45–61. Available: http://w3.coh.arizona.edu/awp/AWP12/AWP12%5BAskildson%5D.pdf

Becker, H. J., & Epstein, J. L. (1982). Parent involvement: A survey of teacher practices. *The Elementary School Journal, 83*(2), 85–102.

Bempechat, J. (1998). *Against the odds: How "at-risk" students exceed expectations.* San Francisco: Jossey-Bass.

Bempechat, J., London, P., & Dweck, C. (1991). Children's conceptions of ability in major domains: An interview and experimental study. *Child Study Journal, 21,* 11–36.

Blackwell, L., Trzesniewski, K., & Dweck, C. S. (2007). Implicit theories of intelligence predict achievement across an adolescent transition: A longitudinal study and an intervention. *Child Development, 78*(1), 246–263.

Bridgeland, J. M., Dilulio, J. J., Streeter, R. T., & Mason, J. R. (2008). *One dream, two realities: Perspectives of parents on America's high schools.* Washington, DC: Civic Enterprises & Peter D. Hart Research Associates.

Broaders, S. C., Wagner Cook, S., Mitchell, Z., & Goldin-Meadow, S. (2007). Making children gesture brings out implicit knowledge and leads to learning. *Journal of Experimental Psychology: General, 136*(4), 539–550.

Catsambis, S. (2001). Expanding knowledge of parental involvement in children's secondary education: Connections with high school seniors' academic success. *Social Psychology of Education, 5*(2), 149–177.

Christenson, S. L., & Sheridan, S. M. (2001). *Schools and families: Creating essential connections for learning.* New York: Guilford Press.

Clark, R. (1993). Homework-focused parenting practices that positively affect student achievement. In N. F. Chavkin (Ed.), *Families and schools in a pluralistic society* (pp. 85–105). Albany: State University of New York Press.

Cochran, K. F. (1997). Pedagogical content knowledge: Teachers' integration of subject matter, pedagogy, students, and learning environments. In R. Sherwood (Ed.), *Research matters… to the science teacher* (2nd ed., No. 9702). Manhattan, KS: NARST.

Corbett, D., & Wilson, B. (2000). *I didn't know I could do that! Parents learning to be leaders through the Commonwealth Institute for Parent Leadership.* Lexington, KY: Commonwealth Institute for Parent Leadership. Available: http://www.prichardcommittee.org/Portals/1059/CIPL/cipl_didnt_know.pdf

Correa-Connelly, M. (2004). *99 activities and greetings great for morning meeting… and other meetings, too!* Turners Fall, MA: Northeast Foundation for Children.

Dauber, S. L., & Epstein, J. L. (1993). Parents' attitudes and practices of involvement in inner-city elementary and middle schools. In N. F. Chavkin (Ed.), *Families and schools in a pluralistic society* (pp. 53–72). Albany: State University of New York Press.

Deslandes, R., & Bertrand, R. (2005). Motivation of parent involvement in secondary-level schooling. *Journal of Educational Research, 98*(3), 164–175.

Eccles, J. S., & Harold, R. D. (1993). Parent school involvement during the adolescent years. *Teachers College Record, 94*(3), 568–587.

Epstein, J. L. (2001). *School, family, and community partnerships*, Boulder, CO: Westview Press.

Epstein, J. L., & Dauber, S. L. (1991). School programs and teacher practices of parent involvement in inner-city elementary and middle schools. *Elementary School Journal, 91*(3), 291–305.

Epstein, J. L., Sanders, M. G., Sheldon, S. B., Simon, B. S., Clark Salinas, K., Rodriguez Jansorn, N., Van Voorhis, F. L., Martin, C. S., Thomas, B. G., Greenfeld, D. G., Hutchins, D. J., & Williams, K. J. (2009). *School, family, and community partnerships: Your handbook for action* (3rd ed.). Thousand Oaks, CA: Corwin Press.

Epstein, J. L., & Van Voorhis, F. L. (2001). More than minutes: Teachers' roles in designing homework. *Educational Psychologist, 36*(3), 181–193.

Farkas, S., Johnson, J., & Duffett, A. (1999, March 17). *Playing their parts: Parents and teachers talk about parental involvement in public schools.* New York: Public Agenda. Available: http://www.publicagenda.org/reports/playing-their-parts

Ferlazzo, L. (2009, May 19). Parent involvement or parent engagement? [blog post]. Retrieved from Public School Insights at http://www.publicschool-insights.org/LarryFerlazzoParentEngagement

Fredrickson, B. L. (2001). The role of positive emotions in positive psychology: The broaden-and-build theory of positive emotions. *American Psychologist, 56*(3), 218–226.

Gardner, H. (1993). *Multiple intelligences: The theory in practice.* New York: Basic Books.

Glasser, W. (1998). *Choice theory in the classroom.* New York: Harper.

Goldin-Meadow, S., Wagner Cook, S., & Mitchell, Z. A. (2009). Gesturing gives children new ideas about math. *Psychological Science, 20*(3), 267–272.

Good, T., & Brophy, J. (2000). *Looking in classrooms* (8th ed.). New York: Longman.

Goodman, J. (1995). *Laffirmations: 1001 ways to add humor to your life and work.* Deerfield Beach, FL: Health Communications.

Harris, J. R. (2009). *The nurture assumption: Why children turn out the way they do.* New York: Free Press.

Henderson, A. T., & Berla, N. (1994). *A new generation of evidence: The family is critical to student achievement.* St. Louis: Danforth Foundation; and Flint, MI: Mott (C.S.) Foundation.

Hodges, L. (2004). Increasing student and school achievement through parent involvement. *Education Update, 10*(1), 25.

Holland, D., Lachicotte, W., Jr., Skinner, D., & Cain, C. (2001). *Identity and agency in cultural worlds.* Cambridge, MA: Harvard University Press.

Hoover-Dempsey, K. V., & Sandler, H. M. (1995). Parental involvement in children's education: Why does it make a difference? *Teachers College Record, 97*(2), 310–331.

Kennelly, B. (2004). *Familiar strangers: New and selected poems 1960–2004.* Tarset, UK: Bloodaxe Books.

Kriete, R. (2002). *The morning meeting book.* Greenfield, MA: Northeast Foundation for Children.

Lane, K. L., Pierson, M. R., & Givner, C. C. (2003). Teacher expectations of student behavior: Which skills do elementary and secondary teachers deem necessary for success in the classroom? *Education & Treatment of Children, 26*(4), 413–430.

Leal, P. (1993). Learn English with a smile. *Actas de las IX Jornadas Pedagogicas para la Enseñanza del Inglís, Granada,* 316–323.

Lee, S. (1994). *Family-school connections and students' education: Continuity and change of family involvement from the middle grades to high school.* Unpublished doctoral dissertation, Johns Hopkins University, Baltimore, MD.

Levine, M. (2003). *The myth of laziness.* New York: Simon & Schuster.

Manke, M. (1997). *Classroom power relations.* Mahwah, NJ: Lawrence Erlbaum Associates.

Mapp, K. (2002). Having their say: Parents describe how and why they are involved in their children's education. *The School Community Journal, 13*(1), 35–64.

McArdle, J. L., Numrich, A. P., & Walsh, K. E. (2002). *Empowering students through the use of the democratic classroom.* Master of arts action research project, Saint Xavier University.

MetLife (2006). *The MetLife survey of the American teacher: Expectations and experiences: A survey of teachers, principals, and leaders of college education programs.* (ERIC No ED496558).

Miedel, W. T., & Reynolds, A. J. (1999). Parent involvement in early intervention for disadvantaged children: Does it matter? *Journal of School Psychology, 37*(4), 379–402.

Mogel, W. (2001). *Blessings of a skinned knee: Using Jewish teachings to raise self-reliant children*. New York: Penguin Books.

Mordkowitz, E., & Ginsburg, H. (1987). Early academic socialization of successful Asian-American college students. *Quarterly Newsletter of the Laboratory for Comparative Human Cognition, 9*(2), 85–91.

Nall, S. (2002). *It's only a mountain: Dick and Rick Hoyt, men of iron* (2nd ed.). Murfreesboro, TN: Southern Heritage Press.

Nater, S., & Gallimore, R. (2005). *You haven't taught until they have learned: John Wooden's teaching principles and practices*. Morgantown, WV: Fitness Information Technology.

National Network of Partnership Schools. (2004). *Taking school home*. Climate of Partnerships publication. Baltimore, MD: Johns Hopkins University.

National PTA. (2005). National PTA/Ad Council "Know More, Do More" campaign. Available: http://www.michiganpta.com/download/Facts/CampaignFactSheet.pdf

Nord, C. W., Brimholl, D. A., & West, J. (1997). *Fathers' involvement in their children's school*. Washington, DC: U.S. Department of Education, National Center for Education Statistics.

Ogle, D. M. (1986). K-W-L: A teaching model that develops activity reading of expository text. *Reading Teacher, 39*, 564–570.

Patrikakou, E. N. (2004). *Adolescence: Are parents relevant to students' high school achievement and post-secondary attainment?* (Family Involvement Research Digest). Cambridge, MA: Harvard Family Research Project. Available: http://www.hfrp.org/publications-resources/browse-our-publications/adolescence-are-parents-relevant-to-students-high-school-achievement-and-post-secondary-attainment

Phillips, D. A. (1987, April 21). *Parents as socializers of children's perceived academic competence*. Paper presented at the biennial meeting of the Society for Research in Child Development, Baltimore, MD.

Ragsdale, S., & Saylor, A. (2007). *Great group games: 175 boredom busting, zero-prep team builders for all ages*. Chicago: Search Institute Press.

Redding, S., Langdon, J., Meyer, J., & Sheley, P. (2004). *The effects of comprehensive parent engagement on student learning outcomes*. Paper presented at the annual meeting of the American Educational Research Association, San Diego, CA. Available: http://www.gse.harfvard.edu/hfrp/projects/fineresourcesreasearch/redding.html

Renzulli, J., & Reis, S. (2007). *Enriching curriculum for all students* (2nd ed.). Thousand Oaks, CA: Corwin Press.

Rich, D. (2008). *MegaSkills: Building our children's character and achievement for school and life*. Naperville, IL: Sourcebooks.

Ridnouer, K. (2006). *Managing your classroom with heart: A guide for nurturing adolescent learners.* Alexandria, VA: ASCD.

Seckel, A. (2005). *SuperVisions: Ambiguous optical illusions.* New York: Sterling.

Seckel, A. (2009). *Optical illusions. The science of visual perception.* Buffalo, NY: Firefly Books.

Simon, B. S. (2001). Family involvement in high school: Predictors and effects. *National Association of Secondary School Principals Bulletin, 85*(627), 8–19.

Siraj-Blatchford, I., Sylva, K., Muttock, S., Gilden, R., & Bell, D. (2002). *Researching effective pedagogy in early years.* Research Report RR 356. Institute of Education, University of London.

Sousa, D. A. (2005). *How the brain learns.* Thousand Oaks, CA: Corwin Press.

Stiggins, R., & Popham, W. J. (2008). *Assessing students' affect related to assessment for learning.* Washington, DC: Formative Assessment for Teachers and Students (FAST) State Collaborative on Assessment and Student Standards (SCASS) of the Council of Chief State School Officers (CCSSO).

Tamis-LeMonda, C. S., & Cabrera, N. (1999). Perspectives on father involvement: Research and policy. *Social Policy Report, 13*(2), 1–32.

Tomlinson, C. A. (1999). *The differentiated classroom.* Alexandria, VA: ASCD.

Trachtenberg, S. (1980). Joke telling as a tool in ESL. *English Teaching Forum, 18*(4), 8–13.

Trelease, J. (1992). *Hey! Listen to this: Stories to read aloud.* New York: Viking.

Trelease, J. (1993). *Read all about it: Great read-aloud stories, poems, and newspaper pieces for preteens and teens.* New York: Penguin Books.

Ueland, B. (1993). *Strength to your sword arm: Selected writings.* Duluth, MN: Holy Cow! Press.

U.S. Department of Education. (2002). *Twenty-fourth annual report to Congress on the implementation of the Individuals with Disabilities Education Act.* Washington, DC: Author. Available: http://www2.ed.gov/about/reports/annual/osep/2002/index.html

Wang, N., Johnson, W., Mayer, R., Rizzo, P., Shaw, E., & Collins, H. (2008). The politeness effect: Pedagogical agents and learning outcomes. *International Journal of Human Computer Studies, 66*(2), 98–112.

Weiner, B. (1994). Integrating social and personal theories of achievement striving. *Review of Educational Research, 64*(4), 557–573.

Weiner, B., Graham, S., Stern, P., & Lawson, M. (1982). Using affective cues to infer causal thoughts. *Developmental Psychology, 21*, 102–107.

Westat & Policy Studies Associates. (2001). *The longitudinal evaluation of school change and performance (LESCP) in Title I schools.* Washington, DC: U.S. Department of Education, Office of the Deputy Secretary, Planning and Evaluation Service.

Yazzie-Mintz, E. (2006). *Voices of students on engagement.* Bloomington: Center for Evaluation and Education Policy, Indiana University.

Index

The letter *f* following a page number denotes a figure.

About the Author

Photo by Mitchell Kearney

Katy Ridnouer teaches with the intention of giving students the tools they need to articulate their unique voices. She does this by creating strategies that help students lift the veils that block efficient learning so that they may use their strengths, cope with their weaknesses, and become successful learners. She has taught in a variety of settings, including public middle and high schools; a private school for students with learning difficulties; a GED program for adult women on the Cheyenne River Reservation in South Dakota; a tutoring center specializing in treating students with learning difficulties; a private school in Dublin, Ireland; and at Central Piedmont Community College, her current position.

Katy earned a Bachelor of Arts degree in English and a Master of Education degree at George Mason University in Fairfax, Virginia. She is the author of *Managing Your Classroom with Heart,* published by ASCD in 2006. She lives in Charlotte, North Carolina, with her husband and three sons. You may contact her at katy@ridnouer.com.

Related ASCD Resources: Student and Parent Engagement

At the time of publication, the following ASCD resources were available (ASCD stock numbers appear in parentheses). For up-to-date information about ASCD resources, go to www.ascd.org. You can search the complete archives of *Educational Leadership* at http://www.ascd.org/el.

Print Products

The Big Picture: Education Is Everybody's Business by Dennis Littky with Samantha Grabelle (#104438)

Inviting Students to Learn: 100 Tips for Talking Effectively with Your Students by Jenny Edwards (#110015)

Managing Your Classroom with Heart: A Guide for Nurturing Adolescent Learners by Katy Ridnouer (#107013)

Mobilizing the Community to Help Students Succeed by Hugh B. Price (#107055)

The Motivated Student: Unlocking the Enthusiasm for Learning by Bob Sullo (#109028)

Motivating Black Males to Succeed in School and in Life by Baruti K. Kafele (#109013)

The Soul of Education: Helping Students Find Connection, Compassion, and Character at School by Rachael Kessler (#100045)

Video and Mixed Media

Creating a Healthy School Using the Healthy School Report Card: An ASCD Action Tool by David K. Lohrmann, Theresa Lewallen, and Pamela Karawasinki (#705191)

Educating the Whole Child: An ASCD Action Tool by John L. Brown (#709036)

The How To Collection: Opportunities for Parent Involvement (five 15-minute video programs on one 96-minute DVD) (#606143)

How to Conduct Home Visits (one 15-minute DVD) (#608030)

How to Involve All Parents in Your Diverse Community (one 15-minute DVD) (#607056)

THE WHOLE CHILD The Whole Child Initiative helps schools and communities create learning environments that allow students to be healthy, safe, engaged, supported, and challenged. To learn more about other books and resources that relate to the whole child, visit www.wholechildeducation. org.

For more information: send e-mail to member@ascd.org; call 1-800-933-2723 or 703-578-9600, press 2; send a fax to 703-575-5400; or write to Information Services, ASCD, 1703 N. Beauregard St., Alexandria, VA 22311-1714 USA.